# High-Impact
# Interview
# Questions

# High-Impact Interview Questions

## 701 Behavior-Based Questions to Find the Right Person for Every Job

### Victoria A. Hoevemeyer

Foreword by Paul Falcone, author of
*96 Great Interview Questions to Ask Before You Hire*

American Management Association

New York • Atlanta • Brussels • Chicago • Mexico City • San Francisco
Shanghai • Tokyo • Toronto • Washington, D.C.

This publication is designed to provide accurate and authoritative information in regard to the subject matter covered. It is sold with the understanding that the publisher is not engaged in rendering legal, accounting, or other professional service. If legal advice or other expert assistance is required, the services of a competent professional person should be sought.

Library of Congress Cataloging-in-Publication Data

Hoevemeyer, Victoria A.
    High-impact interview questions : 701 behavior-based questions to find the right person for every job / Victoria A. Hoevemeyer.— 1st ed.
      p.  cm.
    Includes bibliographical references and index.
    ISBN-10: 0-8144-7301-6
    ISBN-13: 978-0-8144-7301-6
    1. Employment interviewing.   2. Psychology, Industrial.   I. Title.
  HF5549.5.I6H59   2006
  658.3'1124—dc22

                                      2005008487

Printing number

10  9  8  7  6  5  4  3  2

THIS BOOK IS DEDICATED
TO THE MEMORY OF MY GRANDMOTHER,
DOROTHY CAROLINE HISER.

# Contents

# Foreword

**The concept of behavior-based interviewing** has been around for some time now, but nowhere is the art and technique developed as well as in Victoria Hoevemeyer's *High-Impact Interview Questions: 701 Behavior-Based Questions to Find the Right Person for Every Job*. Finally an entire text is dedicated to the critical task of framing interviewing questions around candidates' real life experiences—questions that will prompt factual answers, and focus on future competencies and abilities.

Interviewing has never been a simple process, primarily because we all know how hard people can be to read. Many job candidates are well-studied interviewers but their performance, once hired, may not coincide with the superstar/hero figure they portrayed during initial evaluation. So much rides on hiring the right people—team camaraderie, group productivity, and a positive work environment—that one poor decision could indeed set you and your team back significantly. It's not even uncommon to see managers who tend to leave positions unfilled for long periods of time for fear of hiring someone who doesn't fit in.

Fair enough, but we can't lead our business lives by avoidance or fear of making mistakes. If it's true that the productivity of human capital is the only profit lever in today's knowledge-based economy, then we've got to hire the best and brightest, and develop them to their fullest potential. Your front-end "people reading" skills and selection abilities, therefore, will remain one of your most important portable skill sets as you advance in your own career.

Even if you're not totally comfortable now with your abilities in this area, fear not! Interviewing to make "high probability" hires (remember, no one's asking for "guarantees" when it comes to people forecasting) is a learnable skill. With just a little focus and commitment on your part, you can develop an interviewing routine that's uniquely yours. And employing a behavior-based interviewing format based on the competencies you value and hold dear will give you greater confidence in your abilities to spot talent, which, in turn, will result in stronger hires (which, in turn, further strengthens your confidence!).

Behavioral interviewing is based on real analysis of historical on-the-job performance. Victoria Hoevemeyer's new book makes it so much easier to get to know the real candidate by providing you with competency-based questions for specific scenarios. Whether you're looking to identify corporate-wide competencies or job-specific competencies in a prospective new hire, you'll find behavioral questions specific to multiple scenarios.

The premise is simple: Behavioral interview techniques attempt to relate a candidate's answers to specific past experiences and focus on projecting potential performance from past actions. By relating a candidate's answers to specific past experiences, you'll develop a reliable indicator of how that individual will most likely perform in the future. Behavioral interview questioning strategies do not deny that people can learn from their mistakes and alter their behaviors. However, they do assume that future behavior will closely reflect past actions.

Furthermore, behavior-based questioning techniques ensure spontaneity since candidates can't prepare for them in advance.

Rehearsed answers to traditional interview questions go by the wayside in an ad hoc environment where candidates tell stories about their real life work performance. And because behavioral interview questions tie responses to concrete past events, candidates naturally minimize any inclination to exaggerate answers. Hence, you're assured of more accurate responses during your interview, and you're provided with specific information to use a little later down the line when checking references.

The unpredictable course of behavior-based interviewing exchange may sound something like this:

You:        Tell me what you like least about being a manager at your current company.

Candidate:  Oh, it's definitely having to discipline, lay off, or terminate employees for poor performance. We've had a lot of restructuring in the past year or so.

You:        Sure, that's understandable. I agree that's no fun. *Tell me about the last time that you had to* terminate someone for cause: What were the circumstances, and how did you handle it?

Candidate:  Well, the most recent term for cause in my group happened about four months ago when a member of my staff just couldn't or wouldn't focus on his job. He made continuous errors on the manufacturing line, and it seemed like no amount of training or supervision could get him to focus on his work and lessen the breakage and scrap rate he was experiencing.

You:        Oh, that's too bad. So tell me more about it.

Candidate:  Well, I first went to the union steward and gave her a tip that he was having continuous problems because I knew that they were friends and that he trusted her. I thought she might be able to help him and quietly find out what was really bothering him. I also asked her to give him the Employee Assistance Program (EAP) brochure to make sure he had resources available to help him if personal issues in his life were getting in the way. Unfortunately, she came back to me a few days later, and said he "wouldn't let her in" either. Then she reminded me that since she was a union steward, she really couldn't be involved any further in any activities that could have negative ramifications for a union member, which I fully understood.

You:          Interesting. What was your next step?

Candidate:   Well, I then decided to go straight to the employee with his prior year's performance appraisal in hand. He had scored 4 out of 5, meaning that he had really done well, and I told him that I couldn't give him a 4 if I had to grade him right now. I honestly told him that if the performance evaluation period were right then and there, he'd probably get a score of 2, meaning that he didn't meet company expectations. I told him the good news, though, was that it wasn't the time for the annual evaluation, and that it wasn't too late to turn things around. I just wanted to know if and how I could help. Unfortunately, he wouldn't open up to me either, so we just left it at that.

You:          Did he realize he was heading down a path of termination?

Candidate:   He certainly did. In fact, I ended that meeting letting him know that my door was always open if he needed anything, but that if there were any more problems with excessive breakage and scrap rate, I'd have no choice but to go to Human Resources and look into writing him up for substandard job performance. He even seemed apathetic when I said that.

You:          So it sounds like you were very fair and open with him. *What is it about you* that made you want to speak with the union steward and employee first before going to Human Resources to initiate disciplinary action?

And so the story goes. What's important in this exercise is to see how comfortable and fluid the interview went. It was more of a discussion and "getting to know you" meeting rather than a formal, structured Q&A session with rote responses to one-dimensional questions. The key to a good interviewing style lies in making candidates feel comfortable enough (occasionally) to admit, "Well, I really wouldn't typically say this in an interview, but since I'm so comfortable with you, and since you're asking, I'll tell you. . . ." If you can establish rapport quickly and really help the candidate feel like she could put her guard down because you're both trying to decide *together* if this opportunity is a right fit, then your interviewing skills will leapfrog past your competition, and you'll develop a reputation as a caring and concerned leader. After all, the leadership factor should always come in to play during the very first interview.

In addition, it's always healthy to add self-appraisal questions to your behavior-based questioning techniques that add an honest and somewhat "negative" dimension to the candidate's responses. You can do that by simply using probing or follow-up questions. So your conversation might continue with additional queries like these:

- How would you handle it differently if you could do it all over again?
- Could you argue that you either "jumped the gun" or waited too long to initiate progressive disciplinary action?
- How would your boss grade you on how you handled this deteriorating performance situation in terms of your willingness to confront the problem head on?
- In retrospect, was going to the union first a mistake? What kinds of downsides could it have caused?
- What did the union say in the grievance process about your supervision in its arguments to either avoid termination or to reinstate its member?
- What is it about you that prompted you to handle this situation as you did?

The insights gleaned from this behavior-based interviewing exchange are enormous. The "feel" you now have for this candidate after such a short exchange provides real insights into her approach toward supervision and leadership. What do you now know?

First, she's an open and honest communicator: Her going to the union steward in an effort to provide the employee with support from a trusted friend shows that she's a caring individual who places importance on interpersonal relationships. That being said, any time a manager approaches the union first before going to Human Resources may be a red flag in terms of where the manager's loyalties lie. If her going to the union is an exception based on a known personal relationship between the employee and that particular union steward, then the manager's decision may be understandable. Barring that personal friendship between the employee and the union steward, however, this could be seen as a real area of concern for your company.

Second, the candidate has solid follow-through skills and patience in allowing the union steward a few days' time to resolve the problem.

Third, this interviewee approached her employee in a positive manner—with last year's solid performance review in hand, attempting to motivate the worker by inspiring him to return to a higher performance level.

Fourth, she verbally forewarned the employee that failure to provide immediate and sustained improvement could result in further disciplinary action.

Fifth, when she went to Human Resources as a last resort, the worker surely wasn't surprised, and the interviewee's ultimate decision to work with HR to terminate this individual for substandard job performance demonstrates that she confronts problems head-on, follows protocol, and stands behind her convictions. That's a pretty revealing roleplay, and a great use of your time during the interviewing process!

What also comes into initial play is a focus on the competencies that make someone successful in your organization. In this example, the candidate clearly demonstrates communication and listening skills, human concern, a willingness to confront problems head-on and in spirit of mutual resolution, and the conviction to take punitive action if an employee refuses to rehabilitate himself despite the company's best efforts.

However, although this individual's overall responses may seem positive to you, others may find these same responses unacceptable. For example, some managers believe that going to the union for help—under *any* circumstances—is a mistake because unions and management represent, by definition, opposition. Along the same vein, some managers may feel that a union's presence and effectiveness should be minimized whenever possible so that the company's management team retains as much power and discretion in managing its employees as possible. Still, others may feel that managers should always go to Human Resources first whenever a formal problem arises with a direct report.

Whatever the case, there will always be more room for differing interpretation when candidates respond to interview questions in a behavior-based, "story-telling" fashion. Simply stated, behavior-based questioning techniques provide much more *critical mass* to every interview so that the interviewer has a much more thorough understanding of variances and nuances that could make a big difference in the ultimate decision to hire.

Hoevemeyer's book is structured around hundreds of similar examples using a technique called Competency-Based Behavioral Interviewing, or CBBI. The essence of CBBI is to ensure that a candidate possesses the skills, knowledge, and abilities to be successful in your group. CBBI accomplishes this by amplifying those job-related competencies that are mission critical and unique to your department's success.

More important, you'll find a lot of flexibility in this book in terms of honing in on those competencies, whether by technical performance area or by interpersonal communication ability. So whether you're focused on listening skills or building relationships, writing skills or political savvy, you'll have a host of behavior-based questions at your fingertips, replete with promptings for success stories and failure incidents.

This competency-based interviewing model is about *real* analysis of historical, on-the-job performance. As such, it will set the tone and expectation for integration into other leadership practices as well. The very same competencies that you identify during initial candidate evaluation will dovetail nicely into your performance appraisal, training and development, and compensation and reward systems. And that's the goal—to identify key performers, integrate them smoothly onto your team, set their expectations in terms of what's valued and what will be evaluated, and then help them thrive.

Just remember that it all begins with a consistent, practical interview-questioning paradigm that will save you time, strengthen your candidate evaluation skills, and serve as a successful entrée into your organization's performance management system. Now at your fingertips you have a guiding hand and handy guide to get you there. Enjoy the book, and appreciate the potential that you have to lead, challenge, and motivate those around you.

—Paul Falcone
Author, *96 Great Interview Questions to Ask Before You Hire*

# Acknowledgments

**Thanks to Steve and Lori Hoevemeyer** for their help on the environmental technician telephone-screening interview form. The input on and review of the accounting manager telephone-interview form by Joe Giglio and his accounting team is greatly appreciated. My appreciation also goes to Debbie McQuaide for her attention to detail and her honest feedback on some of this material.

Thanks also to William Miller for his patience, support, and encouragement as he listened to me talk about and brainstorm parts of this book for months and months and months.

Most importantly, I'd like to thank my parents, Kurt and Donna, for their emotional support and encouragement through all my endeavors in life—those they understood, as well as those they didn't.

# Introduction

**If there is one thing** almost everyone who has conducted an interview can agree on it's probably that they would rather have every tooth in their head extracted without the benefit of anesthesia than conduct an interview. OK, so it's probably not quite that bad. But, most people don't like conducting interviews (with the possible exception of those individuals who believe they have an innate talent for interviewing). One of the reasons people have given me for disliking interviewing is that they are already so overworked that they see interviewing as just another imposition on their already over-full schedule. They wish there were a way to make the whole interviewing process go away.

The recruitment process is one of the most important tasks any hiring manager will undertake. Unfortunately, very few hiring managers have ever been taught how to perform this critical task well, which is probably why so many dislike having to do it.

A bad hiring decision will not only affect the hiring manager directly, but may also have repercussions throughout the entire organization. At the very least, a bad hiring decision has the potential of:

1

- Negatively impacting the hiring manager's day-to-day operations

- Playing a critical role in determining his team's ability to achieve their annual goals and objectives

- Creating havoc with other tactical and strategic directives

The impact a bad hiring decision has on others cannot be ignored either. Within the organization, it can lead to aggravated or irritated coworkers, low morale, and additional training time. A bad hiring decision can also have a negative impact on customer service—and potentially even on customer retention. And this does not take into account the time and other resources that could be lost if the employee needs to be terminated and the time that will need to be invested in filling the position again.

I wish I could say that this book is going to take all of the pain out of interviewing, or that it will result in a great hire every time. Unfortunately I can't say either of those. What I can say is that this book will provide some anesthesia to the pain of the interviewing process. The anesthesia comes in the form of competency-based behavioral interviewing (CBBI)—which is not anywhere nearly as cumbersome, intimidating, or complicated as it may sound.

CBBI is simply a structured interview process that focuses on gathering specific, job-related, real-world examples of behaviors the candidate has demonstrated on previous jobs. Because of its focus on competencies, CBBI minimizes the impact of personal impressions that often result in bias during the interview and, as a result, in subjective hiring decisions. The focus of CBBI is not only on matching the candidate with the technical, special, and functional skills required for the position, but ensuring the candidate possesses the competencies for success in the position and the organization.

While this book examines a variety of issues relative to the recruitment process (e.g., telephone screening interviews, making the hiring decision), the focus of the book is on the CBBI questions themselves. This is because one of the primary reasons people cite for not using CBBI is the difficulty in coming up with good, relevant, appropriate questions. This book takes the time, confusion, and complication out of the equation. Once the competencies for the position are determined, it is simply a matter of turning to the list of sample questions for that competency and selecting the question(s) that best solicit the type of information you need on that competency to determine whether or not the candidate is a good fit.

So, if you are looking for new or better ways to predict the on-the-job performance of candidates, to reduce the percentage of "bad hires," or simply to enhance your current competency- or behavior-based interviewing process, you've come to the right place.

# CHAPTER 1

# Interviewing: The Way It Is (Warts and All)

**Behavior-based interviewing,** or competency-based interviewing, has been used in some organizations for as long as twenty-five years. Most organizations, however, continue to use a traditional interview format, which is sometimes interlaced with situational (also called scenario, hypothetical, or "what if") interview questions. The new kid on the block that is making its way into interviewing is the brain twister interview question.

Before getting into competency- or behavior-based interviewing, let's start by taking a look at each of the other interviewing techniques.

## Traditional Interview Questions

Almost everyone is familiar with traditional interview questions. This would include questions such as:

- Do you prefer to work alone or in a group?
- What are your greatest strengths or weaknesses?
- What did you enjoy most/least about your last position?
- How would you describe yourself as a person?
- What kind of books and other publications do you read?

- Where do you want to be in five years?
- Why should I hire you?
- How well do you work under pressure/stress/tight dead-lines?
- How would your coworkers or supervisor describe you?
- Describe the best boss you've ever had.
- Walk me through your work history.

From an interviewer's standpoint, far too many of us can, in our sleep, ask these types of questions. And we are so familiar with the answers that we can almost recite them word-for-word with the candidate.

From a candidate's perspective, there are not many people who have interviewed for a position who have not been asked most—if not all—of these questions. While there are some candidates who find comfort in these types of questions because they have pat answers for them, many are frustrated because they feel that their true strengths and potential contributions are not coming through.

### And Their "Unique" Offspring

I would be remiss if I failed to talk about a variation of the traditional interview question. It is a subcategory of questions that I kindly refer to as "unique." This includes questions such as:

- Who are your heroes and what makes them your heroes?
- If you could be any animal in the jungle, which one would you be and why?
- If you were given a free full-page ad in the newspaper and had to sell yourself in six words or less, how would the ad read?
- If you could invite three people—living or dead—to lunch, whom would you invite and why?

- If you were a bicycle, what part would you be?
- If you had unlimited time and financial assets, what would you do?
- What is your favorite color and what does it reflect in your personality?
- If you were on a merry-go-round, what song would you be singing?
- If your life had a theme song, what would it be?

There are hiring managers who seriously extol the virtue of questions like these. They swear that the candidate's answers will provide significant insights. By asking such questions, proponents say, they will find out how creative a person is, gain an understanding of the candidate's ability to think on his feet, be able to measure his ability to deal with ambiguity, and be able to determine whether he is able to . . . well, you get the idea.

## Advantages of Traditional Interviews

One of the most significant advantages of the traditional interview format is that people understand it and are comfortable with it. While many candidates are nervous going into an interview, the traditional format—since it is a known interviewing approach—will often put them at ease a little faster than other types of interviews.

Second, in most situations, traditional interviews allow for a significant number of questions to be asked in a relatively short period of time. Many traditional interview questions require short answers (e.g., "What are your strengths?"). Even for those questions that require a longer answer, the answer tends not to exceed thirty seconds.

Finally, some traditional questions may reveal fit or non-fit with the position (e.g., "What would your ideal job look like?"), the position's manager (e.g., "What are you looking for in a boss?''), or the organization's culture (e.g., "What kind of organization would you like to work for?'').

The only advantages in sprinkling your interview with "unique" interview questions is that they may help you gauge whether the candidate is able to keep a straight face when confronted with something completely unexpected, and determine whether (but not the extent to which) she can think on her feet.

What's the problem with "unique" questions? The reality is that these kinds of questions have nothing even remotely to do with the candidate's ability to do the job. They are simply silly, time-wasting questions. Any "insight" an interviewer gains from asking such questions is purely conjecture and supposition. There is no research to indicate that any true predictive value has been found in these questions.

Further, by asking such "unique" questions you may just put off a strong, highly qualified candidate. There is a relatively large pool of high quality candidates who would question whether they really want to work for a company that uses a person's favorite color as the basis of any part of a hiring decision.

These are not, by the way, obscure questions I made up. Each and every one of the questions listed above really have been asked of candidates during an interview.

### What's the Problem with Traditional Interviews?

The major problem with traditional interview questions is that virtually every one of them has become a cliché. There are thousands of books and Web sites that provide candidates with the "right" answer to the "top 100 interview questions." The really creative candidates will also purchase the books and go to the Web sites designed for recruiters and hiring managers. They have found that these resources will provide them with "what to look for when the candidates answers question X." This information, then, enables them to fine-tune their perfect answers to each of your questions.

Ask most hiring managers which candidate truly stood out in a series of interviews for a particular position, and you are likely to get a blank stare. The primary reason is that it's hard to distinguish one candidate from another, other than through the eloquence of their presentation. Almost every candidate has memorized—in their own words—the "right" answer to all the questions. As a result, what sends one person to the top of the candidate pile is less likely to be his fit with the competencies required for success in the position and more likely to be the hiring manager's "gut feeling" that the person will be successful.

A final potential issue with traditional interviews is that the same questions are not always asked of every candidate. This raises concerns around how legally defensible many traditional interviews may be, particularly when they are completely unstructured and when the interviewer simply tends to "go with the flow" of each interview and the individual candidate's background.

## Situational Interview Questions

The second type of question you will find in interviews is situational questions, also referred to as scenario-based interviewing, hypothetical questions, or "what-if" questions. In a situational interview, candidates are asked how they would handle a particular situation. In some situations, this is built around a specific scenario (see the 4th through 7th bullet points below). Questions that fall into this category might include:

- What would you do if someone higher than you in the organization instructed you to do something that was unethical or illegal?

- How would you handle a situation where you had conflicting information with which to make a decision?

- How would you handle an employee who was not performing up to expectations?

- Your boss has to leave town to handle an urgent customer problem. He has handed off a project to you that needs to be done prior to his return. The project is for the company's president. Initially you feel your boss has done a good job of briefing you on the project, but as you get into it, you have more questions than answers. You aren't able to reach your boss and you are running out of time. What would you do in this situation?

• A customer brings in a product for repair on Monday. The customer is told that it is a simple repair, and that it would be ready by 3 P.M. on Tuesday. When the customer comes in at 4 P.M. on Tuesday, the product has still not been repaired. The customer is very unhappy. As the service manager, how would you handle the situation?

• You and a coworker are jointly working on a project. The two of you divided up work in a manner you both agreed to; however, your coworker has not been doing the work she agreed to do. What would you do?

• You are a member of a cross-functional team dealing with a difficult problem. The team members have diverse views and sometimes hold very strong opinions or positions. You are constantly in conflict with one of the other team members. How would you establish a satisfactory working relationship with this person to accomplish the team's goals?

What are the advantages of situational interviews? In most situations it is relatively easy to match the candidate's answer to the required answer for the position. For example, if you are looking for a specific six-step process for handling difficult customers, you can check off the steps the candidate lists against the steps used in the organization. This, then, makes it relatively easy to evaluate and rate the answer. You get different information for the candidate who hits only on two of the six steps, than for the candidate who got all six steps but got two of them mixed up in order, or the candidate who lists and explains all six steps in the exact order you have listed.

If you are interviewing entry-level people who may have limited experience, but who have a wide knowledge base, these types of questions may be appropriate. They will, at least, tell you that the candidate knows, intellectually, the process that should be used to address certain situations.

### The Problem with Situational/Hypothetical Questions

The primary problem with hypothetical questions is that they assume that people actually do as they say they will do (or act as they say they will act). This, as we all know, doesn't always happen. For example, I have been facilitating skill-based conflict management programs for about fifteen years. I could walk a trained monkey (and maybe even an untrained one) through the steps. How often do you think I use that process when, after asking three times, I still don't have the information that I asked for in the report. Let me give you a hint: not often!

For many of us there is, unfortunately, very little correlation between knowing the right thing to do or the right process to follow and actually doing the right thing under pressure, while distracted, when in a time crunch, and sometimes even when everything is calm.

Some hiring managers feel that they are able to get around this disconnect by asking a follow-up question like, "Give me an example of when you used this skill or process." And then guess what happens? Almost 100 percent of the time, the candidates' examples will match, letter for letter, word for word, the exact process or skill steps they just described. Does that mean that they practice what they preach? Maybe. But maybe it just means that they are good at putting the "right" process or skill steps into a nice illustrative story and tying it up with a pretty bow for you.

## Brainteaser Interview Questions

The third category of questions is just recently making an appearance in mainstream interviewing. It was "pioneered" by Microsoft and has been used by many of the high-tech companies for a number of years. This category includes questions such as:

- If you could remove any one of the fifty U.S. states, which would it be and why?
- If you stood quarters up on end, how many would you need to equal the height of the Empire State Building?
- What does all the ice in a hockey rink weigh?
- How would you manage a project to get everyone in the United States to drive on the left-hand side of the road?
- Why are manhole covers round?
- How would you weigh an airplane without using a scale?

Proponents of the brainteaser interview questions indicate that these types of questions will provide information on:

- How well the person performs under stress
- The processes the candidate uses to analyze a problem
- How creative or innovative a solution the candidate can come up with
- How intelligent the person is
- How the person reacts to unanticipated challenges or difficult problems

What are the advantages of brainteaser interviews? A hiring manager might want to consider asking a brainteaser question when interviewing a relatively new graduate for a highly technical position. This may give the candidate an opportunity to demonstrate his analytical thinking skills when practical experience is not available.

Another potential advantage of a brainteaser question (not an interview based on them, though) would be the opportunity to gauge a candidate's reaction to the playfulness and innovation that can be inherent in a brainteaser question (assuming, that is, that she enjoys that kind of mental gymnastics). It would also give the interviewer an opportunity to eavesdrop on the candidate's thinking processes.

## The Problem with Brainteaser Questions

There is no problem if you listen to and believe in people like William Poundstone, author of *How Would You Move Mount Fuji,* who says, "If you don't judge people on the basis of something like these puzzles, you're probably going to be judging them on the basis of how firm their handshake is or whether you like how they're dressed, which are even less relevant." However, as quoted in Thad Peterson's Monster.com article, "Brainteaser or Interview Torture Tool," Poundstone also points out that "while various industries have glommed onto this interviewing trend, it makes little sense for many types of workers."

According to proponents, brainteaser questions will tell you how the person thinks, how smart they are, as well as highlight their "rational" and "logical" thinking, planning, and problem-solving and decision-making skills and facilities. It will also, some pundits say, show you how people process information.

Proponents say that these types of questions will lead to creative and original answers that haven't been rehearsed by the candidate. While this may still be the case at this point, there will come a time—most likely sooner than later—when this will not be true. There are an increasing number of books and Internet sites that provide the "right" answer (or the "preferred thought process") for answering many of these questions. It is possible that, in a short period of time, there will be a plethora of candidates interviewing at companies known for using this technique who already know the answers to the questions.

This could lead to an interesting situation. Imagine this situation:

> You ask a candidate a brainteaser question during an interview. Unbeknownst to you, the candidate knows the "right" answer to the question. Because she wants the job, and because she knows she can "fake" thinking through the question out loud, she chooses to play the game and answer the question.

Since you will never know whether the candidate already knew the answer to the question, or whether she was smart enough to figure out the "right" answer, does it cause you to question the value of these types of questions?

I won't argue the point that it is important to understand where a candidate's skill level is and, when appropriate, to know their level of creativity. However, what I have not been able to figure out for the life of me is how someone's answer to "How many piano tuners are there in Chicago?" is going to enable you to determine his fit with the competencies and skill or knowledge requirements for the position. You can, of course, make suppositions and assumptions, but do you really want to hire someone that way?

The ability to solve the brainteaser (to get the right answer, or to answer to the interviewer's satisfaction) may indicate a level of ingenuity, cunning, and even mental dexterity. Whether those are indicators of a candidate's ability to successfully demonstrate the competencies of the position is uncertain. If ingenuity is a competency, the answer may well be yes; if, however, the competency is problem solving, maybe not. For many positions, a candidate's ability to solve a brainteaser may not be a valid and predictive factor for one's successful performance of the position's competencies.

## Stepping Back to the Big Picture

The bottom line is that a big part of the reason these three types of questions continue to dominate organizations is that most managers, when they are asked, are not shy about telling you what good interviewers they are. They say that they have a good "gut reaction" to the answers that candidates provide; they "know in their gut" when someone is "being straight with them." I even had one executive in a service organization tell me (with a straight face) that all she needed to do was look at what the person was doing in the lobby and be able to tell if they were going to work out or not.

Many hiring managers will swear that they get incredible insights into a person when they know things like what the candidate does in her free time and what books she has recently read. (Yes, I have had hiring managers go on and on about all they have learned from candidates' answers to these questions.)

Some hiring managers have gone so far as to tell me that they have virtually "infallible instincts." One manager even told me that he could "smell a bad candidate a mile away," even though his department had a 25 percent turnover rate in an industry that typically had, at the time, about a 10 percent turnover rate.

Unfortunately, hiring on "gut reactions" and "infallible instinct" often does not lead to good hires. More often than not, it results in the hiring manager employing someone just like himself or someone who interviews well rather than someone whose skills and experiences are a best fit for the position and the organization.

The bottom line is this: There is really only one problem with traditional, situational, and brainteaser interview questions: They fail to focus on the demonstrable behavior that will provide sufficient information upon which to determine whether the candidates can do the job for which they are being interviewed.

Before we proceed to the next chapter, it's important to clarify one thing: I'm not saying that you absolutely, positively have to get rid of all of these types of questions in order to have an acceptable interviewing and hiring process. (After all, doing anything "cold turkey" is tough.) What I am recommending is that, if you must use some of them, do three things. First, make them a small minority of the questions you ask rather than the basis of the interview. Second, ask the same questions of every candidate. And third, make the basis of your interview one that is more effective, more predictive, and (if done properly) more legally defensible: competency-based behavioral interviewing.

...................................................

# The What, When, and Why of Competency-Based Behavioral Interviewing

**The primary reason** a company conducts an interview is to learn enough about a candidate to determine whether the person will be successful on the job. There are three parts to this success:

1. Having the technical skills and knowledge
2. Having the functional skills and abilities
3. Being able to demonstrate the position's competencies

The vast majority of interviews focus on the first two components for success; many fail to consider competency proficiency.

When Gillian, the regional manager, interviewed Peter for store manager for a nation-wide retail chain store, she was convinced that fortune was on her side. Peter had extensive budget experience—beyond what was required for the position. He had done scheduling for a number of years and successfully dealt with the challenges of staffing around the holidays. In his last job, he used the same payroll processing company. His business and financial knowledge was thorough—and exemplary. The few minor issues that she uncovered were things that would be addressed as part of the company's New Store Manager Training process. The only reason Peter was looking for a new job was that he was tired of the commute to his current employer, which was one hour each way.

At this point some of you may be thinking, "Anything that sounds too good to be true is probably too good to be true." And you would be right. It took Gillian about a month to go from elated to concerned, and another month to being completely frustrated.

Peter had completed the New Store Manager training program and been in the store for about a month when Gillian started getting calls, e-mails, and letters from customers complaining about Peter. They complained that he was rude, sarcastic, and condescending. Two long-time clerks left within a month of Peter taking over the store, saying, in their exit interview, that they were leaving for more money. Other clerks started leaving shortly after that, making the store's turnover rate twice what it was at other stores.
Gillian sent in a secret shopper whom she had used before and who knew the store and employees fairly well. The secret shopper reported back that morale was through the floor and that when she walked out of the store she was almost as depressed as the employees.

So, what went wrong? As often happens in organizations, Gillian hired a person who was technically and functionally perfect for the position. Unfortunately, Peter was not interviewed against the competencies for success in the position, which included "conflict management," "maintaining a high customer focus," and "building high performance teams." Had he been, he probably would not have been hired.

In the vast majority of positions, the single factor that will distinguish one employee from another is the ability to exhibit the competencies for the position. When you identify and define competencies, and then interview against them—*in addition to* considering the technical and functional aspects—you are increasing the likelihood that the candidate to whom you offer the position is the one who truly is most likely to be successful.

## What Is Competency-Based Behavioral Interviewing?

Before we define competency-based behavioral interviewing (CBBI), it's important that we define a competency. Simply put, a *competency* is a behavior (a skill and/or ability) or set of behaviors that describes the expected performance in a particular work context. The context could be for the organization, a functional job group (e.g., accounting, human resources, operations), a job category (e.g., senior managers, middle managers, professionals), or a specific job. When they are appropriately developed, competencies are the standards of success for the position and the behaviors that are needed to support the strategic plan, vision, mission, and goals of the organization.

Competencies are different from the other requirements one might find for a given position, such as technical skills, functional skills and knowledge, education, and experience. For example, it is one thing to recruit for a position and require five years of management experience. It is another thing to recruit for a position that requires five years of management experience leading a diverse group of people. In the second situation, you would be looking for a candidate with five years of management experience coupled with a demonstrated competency of "valuing diversity."

*Competency-based behavioral interviewing* is a structured interview process that combines competencies with the premise that, with few exceptions:

The best predictor of future performance/behavior is past performance/behavior.

– and –

The more recent the performance/behavior, the more likely it is to be repeated.

The questions asked during CBBI are based on real situations that relate to the competencies for the position. Candidates, then, are evaluated based on actual behaviors/performance rather than on possible or potential behaviors/performance. As a result, the information gathered from the candidate is significantly more predictive of what their behavior and performance are likely to be in the position for which they are interviewing than what one finds with other interviewing styles.

In CBBI, rather than asking candidates directly if they have a particular competency—to which you will almost always hear a resounding "yes!"—the interviewer asks the candidate to provide an example of a time when he demonstrated the competency. The focus is on the candidates giving you an indication of their proficiency in a particular competency by relating a real-world experience.

Typical interviews will sound something like this:

*Interviewer*: "I think I mentioned earlier that this is a high-stress position. How do you manage stress?"

*Candidate*: "My last two positions were high stress. I actually do some of my best work under stress. Through experience, I've learned how to make stress work for me rather than against me. I think two of the most effective stress management techniques are . . ."

Based on the answer the candidate provided, what do you really know about this person's ability to handle stress? Not much— other than the person knows a couple stress management techniques. Whether the person actually uses them or not is up for debate.

What is stressful to this candidate? Your guess is as good as mine. It could be that having to work the rest of the day after getting a paper cut is high stress for this candidate.

Using CBBI techniques, the interviewer would, instead, say something like this:

*Interviewer*: "Tell me about a time you had to perform a task or project under a lot of stress."

Now you are going to find out how the candidate actually handled stress in a real-life situation and what she considers stressful. When used in conjunction with probing/follow-up questions, this question is going to provide significantly more information for comparing candidates to the competency requirements of the position and the culture of the organization than the answer you would receive to the original question. Assuming, that is, that you ensure that the candidate relates a real-life story rather than respond as if you had asked a situational question.

## How Is CBBI Different from Other Interviewing Styles?

When done properly, CBBI is different from the three interview styles discussed in Chapter 1 in at least seven ways.

1. CBBI is designed through a process—beginning with a job, function, and/or organizational analysis—to determine the competencies. Every question asked during a CBBI, then, can be traced back to the initial analysis. The purpose of every question and its contribution to the interview process—and the position—can be clearly and concisely explained. Because of this linked approach, interviewers do not ask irrelevant questions or any question that will not provide specific job-related, competency-based information.

2. Interview questions are planned and directly tied to the competencies for success in the position. A CBBI has specific questions that each interviewer will ask of each and every candidate for the position. This does not mean that there is no flexibility to delve into the candidate's experiences in more detail or get further clarification on something the candidate has said or insinuated. It simply means that every candidate is asked the same initial questions. Follow-up or probing questions will most likely vary from candidate to candidate.

3. Interviewers are trained on the CBBI process. When interviewers receive the training and guidance they need to be good,

thorough interviewers, their confidence goes up, their ability to listen well increases, and they are more likely to reach an objective decision.

4. Rating scales are provided to minimize the subjectivity of the interviewing process. When the levels of proficiency for a competency are clearly defined, there tends to be less debate (or argument) between interviewers in terms of the rating a candidate should receive on a given competency.

5. Interview questions focus on actual current and past behavior rather than "might do" behavior. In most interview situations, a candidate may say, "Were I faced with X situation, I would follow Y process." Unfortunately, you don't know whether the candidate, when called upon to use the process, will actually do what she says. With CBBI, the candidate is telling you exactly and specifically what she did—or didn't—do.

For example, imagine you were hiring a customer service representative. In a traditional interview you might ask, "Have you had to deal with difficult customers in the past?" In a situational interview, you may pose a difficult customer situation and ask, "How would you handle that?" Using a CBBI process, you identified competencies for the position, one of which would (I would hope) be "customer focus." One of the behavioral questions you would ask each candidate then might be, "Tell me about the most difficult customer with whom you have had to deal." The candidate's answer to this question will provide you with two valuable pieces of information that you would not get from the traditional or situational approach.

First, it will tell you what the candidate considers to be an extremely difficult customer. Imagine that *your* most difficult customers would typically make Attila the Hun look like a charmer. Now when you ask the candidate about *his* "most difficult customer," he tells you a story about a customer who is about as difficult as you would expect the Queen of England ever to get (which is not very difficult). In this situation, then, there is probably not a good fit. It is highly unlikely that this person would be able to adequately and appropriately handle the intensity of customer reaction that may be experienced in the position for which he is applying.

Second, the candidate's answer will tell you how he has dealt with difficult customers in the past. In most situations—particularly if it is recent behavior the candidate is sharing—the behavior in the example will most likely be the behavior he will display when dealing with your difficult customers.

6. CBBI makes it easier to compare candidates because they are all measured against the same criteria. These criteria come from the analysis that is conducted at the very beginning of the process. First, they are measured against criteria that can be found on the resume. Those that pass that standard are then measured against the telephone screening interview criteria. Finally, those that pass that standard are then measured during the interview against the same competencies by answering the same questions.

7. CBBI focuses exclusively on competencies that are job-related. It doesn't presume to be able to intuit a person's problem-solving ability (or any other ability) by their answer to a vague question. It does not assume that people who are technical and functionally qualified will necessarily be the best person for the position. CBBI takes a multidimensional approach to hiring. First, it uses technical and functional knowledge, skills, and abilities to narrow the candidate field. Then it uses a focused telephone screening interview to identify the candidates who have the critical skills (non-resume technical and functional expertise, and, in many situations, baseline competencies). Finally, it uses an interviewing process that focuses on the competencies for success in the position to determine the best candidate for the position.

In short, CBBI allows you—the interviewer—the opportunity to gather factual, real-world evidence as to the candidate's ability to appropriately and effectively utilize the competencies required for success in the position and in the organization. As a result, you find out:

1. Whether or not the candidate possesses the required competencies
2. The candidate's skill level on that competency
3. How the candidate is likely to demonstrate his/her skill level in that competency in the future

## Moving to CBBI

While some work is involved in moving from a traditional, situational, or brainteaser format to a competency-based one, the good news is that the format will endure until the competencies for the position change. This means that if you conduct interviews on a quarterly basis for a particular position, you will be able to use the identical interview forms every time, until the competencies for the position change. Even if some of the competencies change, it is a matter of replacing that part of the interview process rather than starting over from scratch.

To make the move, you will need to go through a six-step process:

### Step 1: Determine the Structure for the Competency Model(s)

The first step involves examining the optional competency model approaches and determining the optimal approach for your organization's culture and values. There are, basically, five different approaches an organization can take to establishing competencies.

• *Approach One: Organization-Wide.* This approach would tie into the strategic direction of the organization and would apply to everyone in the organization. The question driving an organization-wide competency model would be, "What are the mission-critical competencies that everyone in this company needs to demonstrate if we are to achieve our strategic plan?" The answers to this question are used as the basis for developing the competency model.

The advantage of this approach is that every employee in the organization is united around a common set of competencies, even though the required level of proficiency may vary. The disadvantage is that, at times, the competencies become so generic and watered down that employees don't understand their importance or value to their day-to-day work lives.

• *Approach Two: Corporate Build.* In this approach, there would be a set of competencies that apply to every individual in the organization. Then, as one goes up the levels in the organization, additional competencies are added. For example, a supervisor would have all of the organizational competencies, plus supervisor competencies; a manager would have all of the organizational competencies and supervisor competencies, plus managerial competencies, and so forth.

This is generally the least time-consuming approach to building an organizational competency model (other than just having a single set of competencies from top to bottom in an organization). It also ties all of the levels in the organization together through a set of common competencies. At times, however, it can result in far too many competencies once one gets to the top management level.

• *Approach Three: By Level.* In this approach, each level in the organization would have a set of competencies unique to that level. The most commonly used division for this approach is

- Hourly
- Office/Professional
- Supervisor
- Management
- Executive

While this approach is sometimes slightly more time consuming than a Corporate Build, there are a couple of reasons that organizations elect to develop their competency model this way. First, it correlates very well with the succession planning methodology of preparing high potentials for any executive level position rather than for a specific position. Another advantage is that it can often result in a more manageable number of competencies more quickly than with a Corporate Build.

The biggest drawback to this approach for some organizations may be the lack of common core competencies throughout the organization. Because of this, some organizations elect to use a Modified Corporate Build approach, where there is a set of four to six organization-wide competencies and four to seven additional competencies specific to the organizational level.

• *Approach Four: By Function/Department.* In this approach, there are competencies established for each function or department in the organization. Everyone in that function or department has the same competencies, regardless of their level or position in the organization. To reflect the fact that the extent of proficiency required for a given competency varies from one position to another, one can apply a weighting factor to each competency on the performance review form (e.g., the level of proficiency on a "continuous improvement" competency would be weighted higher for a manager than for an entry level staff position).

Although the time involved in this approach, and the value it presents to the organization, vary significantly from organization to organization, some organizations find that what it takes to be successful in that organization can be more clearly defined by the function/department than it can be by level. The potential hazard faced in this approach is the tendency to become mired in the task and technical aspects of the function/department rather than focusing on the competencies necessary for success.

• *Approach Five: By Position.* In this approach, competencies are established for each position in the organization. This is, by far, the most time-consuming approach to building a competency model. It is, however, also the most complete, because it focuses specifically on the position. Organizations that use this approach believe that even at a given level in the organization, the competencies for success vary significantly from position to position. That is, for example, the competencies for a Maintenance Supervisor are significantly different from the competencies for a Production Supervisor.

There is no one "best" way to approach the development of competencies. The key to success is to ensure that the approach taken is one that fits with the organization's culture and values, and one that supports the organization's strategic direction.

### Step 2: Determine and Define the Competencies

One of the biggest advantages of following the CBBI process is that you define the competencies for success completely independently of the current employees or potential future candidates. Your focus is on the technical, functional, and special skills, and on the competencies required for success.

Every organization has a different approach for determining competencies. The competencies listed in this book can be used as a starting point for developing individual competency models. There is also a wide range of tools available on the market that will provide guidance in determining the competencies. Regardless of the method or approach used, the competencies need to be clear success factors: competencies that are mission critical to the success of the individual and the organization.

How the competency is defined will also vary from organization to organization. The individual slant that an organization puts on the competency definition is what makes that generic competency unique to their organization. Let's look at some possible definitions for the competency "influencing."

- Presents results-oriented ideas to peers and higher management; able to build relationships that encourage others to support your ideas, make and keep commitments, cooperate with you.

- Able to persuade others; builds consensus through give and take; gains cooperation from others to obtain information and accomplish goals; facilitates "win-win" situations.
- Uses appropriate interpersonal styles and methods to inspire and guide individuals and gain their acceptance of ideas and plans.

While the definitions are similar, each has a slightly different focus. This variation will have an impact on the rating scale used for the competency and on the interview questions asked. Regardless of how the company defines its competencies, the "acid test" will always be that, when asked, a random sample of employees will define a given competency in essentially the same manner.

One thing to consider in establishing competencies, regardless of the method, is focusing on the competencies that will drive the position and the company into the future. For example, imagine a company that has not, in many years, had to be particularly innovative—they have had an enduring product line. The company foresees, however, changes in the market that will require innovation at all levels. As a result, the company establishes a company-wide "creativity and innovation" competency.

For existing employees, they begin offering developmental opportunities (special projects, classroom training programs, e-learning, reading materials, etc.), and begin recognizing and rewarding creative and innovative projects and ideas. For recruitment, a "creativity and innovation" competency is added to the CBBI process. As a result, the company begins to hire people who possess this competency. Now, the company has begun to build a culture of which "creativity and innovation" are a critical part.

### Step 3: Determine the Interview Questions

Typically this is the most arduous part of the process. Fortunately, you were wise enough to purchase this book, making this step relatively simple and straightforward. Simply turn to the page (in

Chapter 3) that lists your competency and, using your own defini-tion of that competency, select the questions you will ask to deter-mine a candidate's proficiency at that competency.

Once you determine the questions, they will be used consis-tently until there is a need to change either a competency or a question within a competency. How these questions are divided up among the interviewers may, however, change. The two vari-ables are the number of people who will be interviewing candi-dates, and how many interviews candidates will need to go through before a hiring decision is made.

If, for example, you have ten competencies, and two questions under each competency, you would have twenty questions. If you have two people interviewing and you will be doing two rounds of interviews before making a selection, you would have each inter-viewer asking five questions during each interview round.

How do you determine which competencies and/or which questions each interviewer will ask? One approach would be to ask the questions associated with the "mission critical" competencies during the first round of interviews, and the questions associated with the remaining competencies during the second round of inter-views. Another possible approach is to ask one question from each competency during the first round of interviews (five per inter-viewer) and the other question from each competency during the second round of interviews.

### Step 4: Develop the Rating Scale(s)

To minimize the variation of ratings from one interviewer to an-other, interviewers can be provided with a rating scale against which to evaluate candidate responses. Chapter 6 explores rating scale options in detail.

### Step 5: Design the Organization's Interview Formats

There are two formats that should be designed if the organization is going to maximize the CBBI process. The first is the telephone-screening interview format. Chapter 5 provides an overview of the purpose of and the process for telephone screening interviews. The second format the organization will need to design is the face-to-face interview, which is discussed in Chapter 6.

### Step 6: Provide Training to All Interviewers

Investing a little bit of money in training interviewers and hiring managers is probably the best investment you can make in your CBBI interviewing and selection process—and for the organization as a whole—to improve interviewer skills and reduce interviewer rating errors. The level and detail of the training goes will depend on how involved the people who will be interviewing are in the development of the interviewing tools. At minimum, the training should cover topics such as:

- How much time to spend on each part of the interview
- Developing a consistent message about the job
- Presenting a company-wide, consistent message about the organization
- How to use rating scales
- Asking questions and listening for STAR answers (STAR stands for Situation, Task, Action, Results; see Chapter 6 for more information on STAR.)
- How to use the telephone-screening interview form
- How to use the face-to-face interview form
- Probing for additional information
- Legal and illegal queries
- Taking notes
- The process for discussing candidates and making a hiring decision

It is also important, as part of the training, for participants (interviewers and hiring managers) to have an opportunity to role

play interviewing. This allows the participants 1
fortable with CBBI, and allows facilitators time 1
playing to ensure that participants are maximiz.. ᵤ
ties for gathering detailed, job-related information.

### A Fast Way to Make the Conversion to CBBI

You do not necessarily need to start with a clean piece of paper if you are going from traditional or situational interviewing to CBBI. Whereas it is best to start by identifying competencies for the position and then selecting behavior-based questions that cover an important aspect of that competency, you can take a shortcut. The shortcut is simply taking your traditional interview questions and converting them to CBBI questions (making sure, of course, that they are legal queries). Some of these conversions are quite simple to do; others may take a little more time and thought. Figure 2-1 provides a few examples.

Although there is no guarantee that converting your traditional questions into CBBI questions will work as well as starting from scratch, chances are that you are going to be getting significantly better, more accurate, more complete, and, well, more behavior-based (or performance-related) information from the candidate upon which to base your hiring decision.

## Objections to CBBI

As with everything, there are people who have specific objections to this type of interviewing. Let's deal with the primary concerns one by one.

1. *CBBI questions are time consuming to develop.*
   Yes, it will take a little time to develop the competencies, define them, select and customize the CBBI questions, and develop the rating scales. However, until the job changes, this will not need to be done again. Even when the job changes, it becomes a matter of

Figure 2-1 Traditional vs. CBBI questions.

| Traditional | CBBI |
|---|---|
| How do you deal with an angry, upset, or irate customer? | We all have to deal with customers who are angry, upset, or even irate. Tell me about the worst situation you have had to deal with. |
| What would you do if someone asked you to do something unethical? | Tell me about a time you were asked to do something that you felt was unethical. |
| If you could change one work-related decision you made during the past year, what would that be? | Tell me about a work-related decision that, if you could, you would like to redo. Why would you want to redo it? What did you learn from the experience that you would apply to the redo? |
| How do you work under pressure? Do you handle pressure well? | Tell me about a time you were faced with stressors at work that tested your coping skills. Tell me about a time you did not handle a stressful situation well. |
| If you could live your life over again, what would you change? | Tell me about a work-related decision you made or a situation you handled where, if you had it to do over again, you would do something different. |
| How would you rate your communication skills and what have you done to improve them? | Give me an example of a time when you were not as successful in your oral communication as you would have liked to have been. What did you learn from this situation that you have used to improve your communication skills? |
| What kind of people do you like to work with (or do you have difficulty working with)? | Describe the way you handled a specific problem involving others with differing values or beliefs. |
| What motivates you to put forth your best effort? | We all get assignments we really don't want to do. Give me an example of a time that happened to you and tell me how you motivated yourself to get it done. |
| How do you go about determining your priorities? | Tell me about a time when you had too many things to do and you were required to prioritize your tasks. |

| | |
|---|---|
| How would you work together on a project with more than two or three people? | Give me an example of a time where you needed to get people who have very different work styles to work cooperatively on a project. |
| What are you most proud of? | Tell me about something you did in your [last/current] position of which you are particularly proud. |
| What process do you use to solve problems? | Give me an example of a difficult problem you faced and how you went about solving that particular problem. |
| What are your strengths? | Describe a time when one of your strengths enabled you to be successful where you might not have been otherwise. |
| If you were a tree, what kind of tree would you be? | OK, I give up! There are simply some questions that can't – or shouldn't – be rephrased! |

tweaking rather than redoing everything. Also, as mentioned earlier, this book eliminates the significant research that needed to be done to come up with appropriate questions in other interview formats.

2. *Word will leak out about the CBBI questions and we'll end up with rehearsed answers.*

It's always a possibility that this could happen. If that is a concern, one up-front solution is to select three to four CBBI questions for each competency and rotate the questions on a regular basis. The worst-case scenario is that you occasionally run into a candidate who has—or sounds like she has—a rehearsed answer. This is where your probing questions can become even more valuable.

It is relatively easy for most people to come up with a "good story," but it's another thing to be able to answer probing questions well and get the pieces to fit together right on a falsified story. When the story is falsified, most people will start demonstrating rather awkward, uncomfortable verbal and/or nonverbal behavior. To distinguish whether this is nervousness or falsification, you can always ask another question or reword the question you just asked from a positive to negative format (for example, from "Tell me a time when you did . . ." to "Tell me about a time when you did not . . .").

3. *These types of interviews take longer.*

Yes, they do. Here are your choices:

*Choice A*: Conduct a quick traditional interview. Since research has shown that they have less than a 30 percent chance of predicting job performance, your chances of making a bad hiring decision for an $80,000-a-year job, for example, are pretty high. Depending upon which reports you read, it costs between 30 percent and 250 percent of a position's annual salary to replace an employee. Let's say the cost to replace the bad hire is 100 percent (simply because it makes calculations easy). So, it will cost you $80,000 to fill that job. With a 70 percent or greater chance that this was a bad hire, you will then have to go through the entire process again, resulting in a cost of at least $160,000 to fill the position (and that's assuming that the second person hired is a good fit).

*Choice B*: Invest time up front to determine the requirements for the position (technical skills, special skills, and competencies), design and conduct a skill and competency-based telephone screening interview, and conduct a CBBI that focuses on competencies and demonstrated behaviors. Research has shown that this approach is upwards of 65 percent effective in measuring and predicting job performance and success as compared to traditional or situational interviews. While you still have $80,000 invested in the hiring decision, you're significantly less likely (less than a 35 percent chance) to be going through the entire recruitment process again in the next few months to replace the new hire.

Yes, traditional, situational, and brainteaser interviewing are, typically, much faster. They are, however, potentially much more expensive.

4. *If we hire technically skilled people with the required background and education, we can train them on the "soft" competency stuff.*

There are positions for which this is true, but why would you want to go to the expense of training people when you could hire them with the competencies already demonstrated at a proficient level? Also recognize that while *some* competencies are relatively straightforward for people to learn through training or on the job (e.g., customer focus, presentation skills, written communication), there are quite a few competencies that are extremely hard to develop (e.g., ethics, innovation, organization, motivating others, or compassion). In addition, if you take the "train them after you hire them" approach, you need to consider that it will take from three to six months for the employee to integrate each new skill into day-to-day behavior. This could result in a significantly long learning curve before he is performing all aspects (technical and functional skills as well as competencies) of the job in a proficient manner.

5. *Behavioral interviewing is too structured and doesn't allow the flexibility to react to individual candidate differences.*

CBBI is a structured process—and one that increases the likelihood (if well developed and followed by the interviewer) of conducting a legal interview. It is not so structured, though, that it does not allow for the interviewer to gather relevant job-related information. The interviewer is free to ask legally appropriate follow-up or probing questions. Many organizations will also allow interviewers to solicit reverse information from a candidate.

For example, imagine that the question in the Interview Guide is, "Give me an example of a time you *really* listened to a person who was telling you about a personal/sensitive situation." The interviewer can ask probing questions to ferret out the details of the situation. Many organizations also allow the interviewer to reverse the question by saying, "Now tell me about a time you failed to listen well to someone telling you about a personal/sensitive situation."

Another example of the flexibility of CBBI is that most organizations will encourage interviewers to explore examples of related competencies that a candidate presents. For example, imagine that you work in a company where there is a competency of "teamwork" and "perseverance." You have asked the candidate a "teamwork" question, and during the response, the candidate talks about the team persevering in the face of multiple setbacks. One of your follow-up questions may be, "You mentioned the team persevering through setbacks. What were the setbacks? What did you do to get your team through these setbacks?"

6. *It takes too long to complete a behavioral interview.*

Yes, it does take more time. But the reason is that you are probing for actual behaviors rather than *hypothetical* answers. Most interviewees are able to come up with a "right" answer to hypothetical situations fairly quickly. They know what they *should* do. They have memorized the process or the procedure. However, people don't necessarily do what they should do or what they say they will do. Determining how people actually behaved in a real situation takes a little more time, but gives you a much richer source of information to determine whether the candidate would be a good match for the job or not.

## Why Use Competency-Based Behavioral Interviewing?

• First of all, CBBI is more valid than traditional interviews. Research shows that it is three to five times more accurate at predicting a person's potential than traditional interviews. With the high cost of hiring (or replacing an employee terminated for a "bad fit"), that can lead to substantial cost savings.

• Second, because CBBIs focus on actual past behavior—behavior that the candidate is highly likely to repeat—you are more apt to get a real-life view of how the candidate will actually perform on the job. This is more likely to result in a successful hire, which means:

- Increased productivity
- Lower turnover
- Higher morale

- Better quality
- Better customer service

• Third, because it is a structured process, it helps interviewers stay on track and minimizes the possibility that the interviewer will ask either planned or spontaneous illegal or inappropriate questions.

• Fourth, when it is done properly, it provides the company with a legally defensible interview process. Because competency-based behavioral interviews are structured and objective, they tend to be more defensible than other types of interviews.

## Key Advantages of Using CBBI

From an *organizational* standpoint, CBBI, when done properly, offers a number of key benefits:

- It establishes an organization-wide, systematic interviewing process that supports the vision, mission, values, and strategic direction of the organization.
- Since competencies are observable and measurable, it allows for the gathering and evaluation of objective performance data.
- It ensures that only relevant, job-specific questions are asked.
- It gathers specific, real-world performance information upon which to base a hiring decision.
- It increases the likelihood that a fair, objective selection will be made.
- It increases the possibility of hiring the candidate who is the best fit for the position and the organization.
- It lowers the organization's legal risks associated with interviews, when properly used.

- It promotes objectivity when used in conjunction with competency-specific rating scales.
- Candidate answers are more honest and natural—rather than pre-planned and memorized—enabling the interviewer to determine more accurately whether the candidate possesses the competencies for success in the position.

From a candidate's perspective as well, there are at least two solid benefits to the use of CBBIs:

1. There is relevance between the questions asked and the position. Even if candidates don't like behavioral questions, they at least see more value in the question than they see in questions like, "If you were a salad, what would you have in you other than lettuce?"

2. Even candidates with limited work experience have had life experiences. For example, when interviewing for a position that requires the competencies of adaptability, initiative, and communication, most people will have had an opportunity outside of work to demonstrate these competencies.

CHAPTER 3 ......................................................

# Competency-Based Behavioral Interview Questions

**This chapter** lists 701 competency-based behavioral interview (CBBI) questions, organized under 78 competencies. Once you have identified the appropriate competencies for the position, level, and your organization, your next step is to develop brief definitions of each competency that take into consideration your organization's culture. Once the definitions have been developed, you can then pick those questions that best determine whether a candidate can demonstrate the competency at the required level for your organization.

Because organizations have slightly different interpretations of what each competency means, the questions listed under each competency, in most cases, span a wide range of factors associated with that competency.

There are also questions that are worded differently but that elicit the same information. This, again, is designed to enhance the organizational fit of the questions to the culture and preferred vernacular of different organizations. It is important to read through each question and select the one(s) most relevant to the position for which you will be interviewing candidates.

## The Missing "Leadership" Competency

When developing competencies for a management level position it is tempting to include a competency called "leadership." In this book, you will not find a competency called "leadership." That is because leadership is an amalgamation of a number of competencies, rather than a single competency. To determine what those competency components are for your organization, ask, "What does a leader do in this organization that puts her above the rest?" The answer may yield comments such as:

- "Recruits the best of the best; isn't afraid to hire people who are more knowledgeable than he is."
- "Is able to get a group of people to work effectively as a team; able to build *esprit de corps*."
- "Is able to get the best out of each of her employees; people go the extra mile for her."
- "Makes good decisions, even when there is insufficient information or little time in which to do so."

These comments are then phrased into individual leadership competencies within the organization. For example, in the above situation, the competencies may be worded like this:

- Hires the best
- Builds an effective team
- Motivates well
- Makes effective decisions

## Soliciting Negative Incidents

Many competencies present questions that can be used to elicit negative incidents as well as positive incidents. In some situations negative—or "failed"—examples of the competency can be of a value equal to or greater than a positive incident the candidate could relate. For example, if the ability to learn from mistakes is extremely important on a particular competency, it might make more sense to solicit the candidate's real-world experience from a "failure" perspective, instead of or in addition to a "success" perspective.

For example, as shown in Figure 3-1, using the success and failure questions together may help you ascertain a candidate's ability to effectively demonstrate the competency of "building a team," as well his ability to pick up the pieces from a failed effort and get the team moving in the right direction.

You may also want to ask a "failure" question when you are getting the feeling that the candidate sounds too perfect. For example, if one of the competencies for Position X is "results oriented," you may say:

"Describe a time when, against all odds, you were able to get a project or task completed within the defined parameters."

Now, imagine that all the answers the candidate has provided thus far have indicated that this is an incredibly strong candidate for the position. You don't believe anyone could be this perfect. You now have the opportunity to re-explore this competency in a contrary manner, saying:

"Now, I would like you to tell me about a time when you were *unable* to get a project or task completed within the defined parameters."

As the candidate answers this question, listen for critical issues. For example:

Figure 3-1  Success and failure questions.

| Competency: "Building a Team" | |
|---|---|
| Positive Incident: | "Give me an example of a time that your leadership transformed a group of people into an effective, healthy, productive team." |
| Negative/Failed Incident: | "Give me an example of a time when you were less successful as a team leader than you would have liked to have been." |

- Were the roadblocks within or outside the person's control?
- What actions did the candidate take to eliminate or get around the roadblocks?
- Did the candidate miss early warning signs?
- How significant was the failure?

# SAMPLE CBBI QUESTIONS

## Action Orientation

1. Tell me about a time you got enjoyment out of working hard on something.

2. Give me an example of a time you had to work on a project/task that you were absolutely dreading.

3. Give me an example of something you've done in previous jobs that demonstrates your willingness to work hard.

4. Describe a challenging project that you worked on.

5. Give me an example of a time that you had to act with very little planning.

6. Tell me about a time that you willingly took on more work even though you were already busy. How were you able to get everything done?

7. We all feel that we are unique in our accomplishments. Tell me an accomplishment you have had that you feel is unique.

8. Sometimes people will drag their feet in taking action on something, losing precious time. Tell me about a time you saw that other people in the organization were not acting quickly on something and took it upon yourself to lead the effort.

## Ambiguity (Ability to Deal With)

1. Tell me about a time you had to work with conflicting, delayed, or ambiguous information. What did you do to make the most of the situation?

2. Tell me about a time when ambiguity was an obstacle to you getting a task or project completed. What was ambiguous? How long was it ambiguous?

3. Give me an example of a time when there was a decision to be made and procedures were not in place. What was the outcome?

4. We have all been asked on occasion to perform a task or accomplish a goal where the instructions we received were ambiguous. Tell me about a time when this happened to you and specifically what you did.

5. Give an example of a time when you could not participate in a discussion or could not finish a task because you did not have enough information.

6. Tell me about a time when you had to complete a project/task on a strict deadline with little or no direction.

## Analytical Skills

1. Tell me about the most complex or difficult information you have had to analyze.

2. Tell me about the task or project that you were responsible for that best demonstrates your ability to analyze information.

3. Sometimes even though we study the data from all sides, we make errors in interpretation of the data. Tell me about a time that happened to you.

4. Give me an example of a time where you caught a discrepancy or inconsistency in the available information that might have caused significant problems if you had missed it.

5. Describe a time where your "logical analysis" was seen as illogical or flawed by someone else.

6. There are times where there is an incredible amount of data and information to be analyzed. Tell me about a time you faced this situation and exactly what you did to boil everything down to what was most important.

## Approachability

1. Tell me about a time when someone came to you with a problem. What did you do?

2. Give me an example of a difficult problem someone recently needed your help to solve.

3. Give me an example of a time an employee came to you and was anxious about something. How did you handle the situation? What was the result?

4. Describe a time when you went out of your way to put someone at ease.

5. Tell me about a time you were able to establish a rapport with a person that others referred to as "difficult."

6. Give me an example of a time that you were provided with information that enabled you to stop a potential problem from occurring.

7. Give me some examples of when someone remembered you after only a brief introduction. Why do you think they remembered you?

## Business Acumen/Understanding the Organization

1. Give me some examples of how people in other parts of the organization use your department or group as a resource.

2. Give me an example of a decision that was made in your area that had an adverse impact on another area or department.

3. Tell me about a decision you made that had an unexpected positive impact on another area or department.

4. Give me an example of a time where your understanding of your organization enabled you to get something you needed that, had you lacked the understanding, you probably would not have gotten.

5. Tell me about a time you recognized a problem before your boss or others in the organization did. What was the problem? What was the result?

6. Describe a time when politics at work affected your job. How did you deal with it?

7. Tell me how you went about learning how your current organization works.

## Career Ambition

1. Tell me about your career plan and what you have done so far to accomplish it.

2. Describe for me how you have "made your own luck."

3. Give me an example of how you have taken control of your career.

4. Give me an example of a time you knew you had outgrown a position and it was time to move on.

5. Tell me about your greatest career achievements. Why did you pick those examples?

6. Tell me about a time you felt "off track" in your career progress.

7. Tell me about a time when you turned down a good job.

## Caring About Direct Reports

1. Give me an example of how you have celebrated an individual's or your team's success in the past. What was the occasion?

2. Tell me about a time when you were able to provide a direct report with recognition for the work she performed. What did you do?

3. Tell me about a time you missed an opportunity to provide a direct report with recognition for a significant accomplishment. Why did you miss it? What did you do when you realized you missed it?

4. Tell me what you have done on a consistent basis to ensure that your direct reports feel valued for their contributions?

5. Describe a time when one of your direct reports was under a great deal of pressure or stress. What did you do in the situation? What was the outcome?

6. Tell me about a time that you sensed that something was wrong with one of your direct reports and talked to him about it. What was the result?

7. Give me an example of a time that you realized that one of your direct reports was overburdened with work. What did you do? How did your action affect the situation?

8. Describe a work situation that required you to really listen and display compassion to a coworker/employee who was telling you about a personal/sensitive situation.

## Change Management

1. Tell me about the most difficult change you have had to make in your professional career. How did you manage the change?

2. Give me an example of a time when you missed the early signs of employee resistance to an organizational change.

3. Describe a time when you felt that a planned change was inappropriate. What did you do? What were the results?

4. Tell me about a time when you had to adapt to an uncomfortable situation.

5. Tell me about a time you led a change effort.

6. Describe a time a change effort you were involved in was not as successful as you or the company would have liked.

7. Give me an example of a time you had to adjust quickly to changes over which you had no control. What was the impact of the change on you?

8. Give me an example of a time when you helped a direct report or other person in the organization accept change and make the necessary adjustments to move forward. What were the change/transition skills that you used?

9. Describe a situation where you, at first, resisted a change at work and later accepted it. What, specifically, changed your mind?

## Comfort Around Higher Management

1. Describe a time you were able to provide a higher level management person with recognition for the work she performed.

2. Tell me about a presentation you made to upper management. What was it about? How did you feel about making the presentation? How did it go?

3. Give me an example of a time where, by speaking management's language, you were able to convince them to do something that they might not have done otherwise.

4. Give me an example of a time where, despite being tense or nervous, you were able to make a successful presentation to a higher level management group.

5. Tell me about a time where, had you taken time to think about how a higher level management person or group liked to receive information, you might have been more successful. If you had it to do over again, what would you do differently?

## Communication (Oral)

*Successful Communication*

1. Tell me about the most difficult or complex idea, situation, or process you have ever had to explain to someone. How did you explain it? Were you successful?

2. Give me an example of a time you had to be excellent at multidirectional communication in order to be successful at something.

3. Describe a time when you had difficulty communicating your thoughts clearly to another person or group. What message were you trying to convey? Where did the difficulty in communicating lie? How did you end up getting your point across?

4. Describe a time you used verbal communication to get across a point that was important to you. Were you successful? How do you know you were successful/unsuccessful?

5. Give me an example of a time when you were able to successfully communicate with another person even when that individual personally may not have liked you.

6. Give me an example of a time when you were able to successfully communicate with a person *you* personally did not like.

7. Describe a time that you were successful primarily because of your ability to communicate orally.

8. Describe a situation where you had to collect information by asking many people a lot of questions.

9. Tell me about a sensitive or volatile situation that required very careful communication.

10. Tell me about a job experience in which you had to speak up in order to be sure that other people knew what you thought or felt.

11. Give me an example of a time when you were able to successfully communicate with another person even when you felt the individual did not value your perspective.

12. Describe a situation you observed or were a part of where communication was handled particularly well by someone else. What did they do? Why do you think it was effective?

*Failed/Misunderstood Communication*

13. Tell me about a time when someone misunderstood something you said. How did you determine that you had been misunderstood? How did you make yourself clear? What did you learn from this situation that you have used to improve your communication skills?

14. Describe a time you failed to communicate important information to your boss.

15. Tell me about a time you failed communicate effectively with your direct reports/client/customer. How did you find out you had failed to communicate effectively? What was the implication of this failure? What did you do about the situation? What did you learn from this?

16. Tell me about a time when your dislike for an individual had a negative impact on your ability to communicate effectively with this person.

## Communication (Written)

1. Give me an example of an important report you have written.

2. Give me an example of the kind of writing you do best.

3. Tell me about a time when someone misunderstood something you wrote. How did you determine that you had been misunderstood? How did you make yourself clear?

4. Tell me about a time in which you had to use your written communication skills in order to get an important point across.

5. Describe the most significant or creative written presentation you had to complete.

6. Tell me about a time when you used your written communication skills to convey an important message.

7. Describe a time you wrote a report that was well received by others.

8. Tell me about a time where you didn't document something that you wish you would have.

9. Give me an example of a time you used written communication to share information that, in hindsight, you realize should have been shared verbally.

## Compassion

1. Give me an example of a time you were particularly perceptive regarding a person's or group's feelings and needs.

2. Describe a time when an employee came to you with a personal pain he was experiencing.

3. Tell me about a time when you demonstrated to a direct report that you were concerned about a work or nonwork problem he was experiencing.

4. Describe a work situation that required you to really listen and display compassion for another person who was telling you about a personal or sensitive situation.

5. Give me an example of a time you had to put a critical task or project you were working on aside to attend to the needs of a direct report.

6. Tell me about a time when your failure to show compassion to someone at work was a costly oversight on your part.

7. Tell me about a time when you needed to give feedback to an emotional or sensitive employee.

8. Give me an example of a particularly difficult or awkward conversation you needed to have with someone.

## Composure

*Positive Incidents*

1. Tell me about a time you took action based on your own convictions rather than giving in to the contrary pressures of others' opinions.

2. Describe the worst on-the-job crisis you had to solve. How did you manage to maintain your composure?

3. Give me a recent example of a situation you have faced when the "pressure was on." What happened? How did you handle it?

4. Give me an example of a time you worked particularly well under a great deal of pressure. How did you handle the situation?

5. Tell me about a time you felt your team was under too much pressure. What did you do about it?

6. Describe a time where you were faced with problems or stressful situations that tested your coping skills. What did you do?

7. Give me an example of a time you had to think quickly on your feet to extricate yourself from a difficult situation.

*Failure Incidents*

8. Tell me about a time you lost your temper/cool/composure.

9. Tell me about a time you were knocked off balance on a project you were working on due to unexpected information or an unexpected event.

*"Testing the Waters"*

10. Think about a time when you felt overwhelmed or stressed out. How did you handle it?

11. Tell me about a time when your work or an idea of yours was criticized.

## Conflict Management

*Positive/Success Incidents*

1. Describe a time when you facilitated a creative solution to a problem between employees.

2. Tell me about a recent success you had with an especially difficult employee or coworker.

3. Describe a time when you took personal accountability for a conflict and initiated contact with the individual(s) involved to explain your actions.

4. Give me an example of a time on the job when you disagreed with your boss or a higher level manager. What were your options for settling the conflict? Why did you choose the option you did? Were you able to get your point across? How successful were you in settling the conflict?

5. Others' work ethics are sometimes in conflict with our own. Describe a time this happened to you. Were you able to work it out? How (or why not)? What did you learn from this experience? How have you applied that learning?

6. Tell me about a disagreement that you found difficult to handle. Why was it difficult? What did you do? How did it work out?

7. Thinking of the most difficult person you have had to deal with, describe an interaction that illustrates that difficulty. Tell me about the last time you dealt with him. How did you handle the situation?

8. Tell me about a time when you and your previous supervisor disagreed but you still found a way to get your point across.

9. Describe a time when you took personal accountability for a conflict and initiated contact with the individual(s) involved to explain your actions.

10. There are always times when we disagree with others. Some people are congenial when we disagree with them, but that's not true of others. Tell me about a time when you had the courage to express your opposing

opinion to someone who generally does not take well to opposing viewpoints. What relationship was this person to you? Why did you decide to
speak up?

11. Describe a time when you had to resolve a conflict between two employees
    or two people on a team.

### Negative/Failed Incidents

12. Tell me about a time you did not properly handle a disagreement with a
    coworker.

13. Tell me about a time when you felt that a coworker or manager made you
    look bad.

### Miscellaneous

14. Think about a time when you were involved in a group project or activity
    where the others involved were difficult to get along with. What did you do
    about it?

15. Tell me about a time you were faced with conflicting priorities. How did you
    resolve the conflict? Was it effective? Why or why not?

## Confronting Direct Report Problems/Issues/Concerns

1. Some people are more difficult to work with than others. Give me an example of how you have worked with the most difficult direct report and how
   that differed from how you worked with the most accommodating direct
   report.

2. Tell me about a confrontation you've had with a direct report.

3. Tell me about a time one of your direct reports was not meeting expectations.

4. Describe for me a time you let a problem with an employee get out of
   hand.

5. Tell me about a time you needed to terminate an employee for performance problems. How long between first determining there was a problem and termination?

6. Give me an example of a time when you had to talk to a direct report about her performance and were able to turn that employee around.

## Continuous Improvement

1. Tell me about a suggestion you made to improve the way job processes/operations worked.

2. Tell me about one of your workplace improvements that another department now uses.

3. Give me an example when you initiated a change in a process or operations.

4. In your last or current job, what problems did you identify that had previously been overlooked? Were changes made? Who supported the changes as a result of your ideas?

5. Tell me about something new or different that you did in your department that improved customer service, productivity, quality, teamwork, or performance.

6. Tell me about a time you found and took advantage of an opportunity to make an improvement in your position or department/team/group.

7. Tell me about a time when you had to sacrifice quality to meet a deadline. How did you handle it?

8. In some aspects of work, it is important to be error free. Describe a situation where you tried to prevent errors.

9. Describe a time you caught an error that someone else made that could have affected the outcome of a project (or affected a customer).

10. Tell me about a suggestion you made to improve the processes or operations in your position or within your team.

11. Give me an example of a time you improved the use of or return on a resource, where the positive impact was broader than just your team/department.

## Cooperation

1. Gaining the cooperation of others can be difficult. Give a specific example of when you had to do that, and what challenges you faced. What was the outcome? What was the long-term impact on your ability to work with this person?

2. Describe a time where, had you not been able to get another person's or group's cooperation, you probably would not have been successful.

3. Tell me about a time that you cooperated with someone when you really would rather have not cooperated.

4. At times, we must all deal with difficult people. This can be a challenge when it is someone with whom we need to develop a cooperative relationship. Tell me about a time you were successful in developing a cooperative relationship with a difficult person at work.

5. What is the toughest group/team/department from which you have had to get cooperation? What were the obstacles? Why was it a tough group? What were the reactions of the group members?

## Courage

1. Describe a time you had to make a decision that you knew would be unpopular.

2. Summarize a situation where you took the initiative to get others going on an important issue, and played a leading role to achieve the results needed.

3. Tell me about a situation when you stood up for a decision you made even though it was unpopular.

4. Describe a leadership situation you would handle differently if you could do it over again.

5. Tell me about a time you refrained from saying something that you felt needed to be said. Do you regret your decision? Why or why not?

6. Give me an example of a time you needed to give constructive feedback to one of your peers or someone higher in the organization about his behavior.

7. Tell me about a time you felt you needed to be assertive in order to get what you felt you or your team deserved or needed.

## Creativity/Innovation

1. A lot of times we use tried-and-true solutions to solve problems and it works. Tell me about a time when the tried-and-true solution did *not* work. Were you able to solve the problem? How? In what way was that solution different from the tried-and-true solution?

2. Describe a time when you came up with a creative solution/idea/project/ report to a work problem you had been dealing with for some time.

3. Tell me about a situation when you have had to come up with several new ideas in a hurry. Were they accepted? Were they successful?

4. Describe a creative/innovative idea that you produced that led to a significant contribution to the success of an activity or project.

5. Describe the most creative work project you've ever accomplished.

6. Tell me about a time you were especially creative in solving a lingering problem.

7. Describe the most significant plan or program that you ever developed or implemented.

8. Tell me about a time when you created a new process or program that was considered risky.

9. Describe the most creative thing you have done in a past job.

10. Creativity often means stepping back from standard ways of thinking. Give me an example of a time when you were able to break out of a structured mindset and explore new or different concepts and ideas.

11. Give me an example of how you have been creative in completing your responsibilities.

12. Tell me about the last time you thought "outside the box." (*NOTE: Make sure they explain both why and how they did it.*)

13. Give me an example of when someone brought you a new idea that was unique or unusual. What did you do?

14. Describe the most creative oral presentation you have ever made.

15. Tell me about a problem that you've solved in a unique or unusual way. Were you happy with the outcome?

## Customer Focus

*Effectively Handling a Difficult/Emotional Customer*

1. Tell me about a time when you did your best to resolve a customer or client concern and the individual was still not satisfied.

2. Give me an example of a time you effectively used your people skills to solve a customer problem.

3. Tell me about a time when you encountered a customer who was complaining of poor service. What did you do?

4. At times, we are all required to deal with difficult people. An even more demanding factor is to be of service to a difficult person. Describe a time you were successful dealing with a difficult customer.

5. Tell me about a time you wished you would have handled an unhappy, angry, or irate customer a different way.

*Building/Enhancing/Preserving Customer Relationships*

6. Give me an example of something you have done to either develop or strengthen customer relationships.

7. Describe for me something you did to established a "customer first" mentality in your department or team.

8. Tell me about a customer whose needs you spent considerable time learning about. What was the result of the time investment?

9. Tell me about a customer who has stuck with you over the years. What did you do to make this happen?

10. Describe the process or method you used in a particular situation to develop an understanding of your internal/external customer's viewpoints and needs.

11. Describe a time you exceeded the expectations of a client/customer/stakeholder.

12. Give me an example of a time when you acted as an advocate for a client or customer in the face of resistance from a person or the organization as a whole.

### Breakdowns in Customer Service

13. Describe a time you were not able to deliver a product or service to your customer on time.

14. Everyone has said something to a customer that they wished they hadn't. Tell me about a time you did this. What did you do to correct the situation?

15. Tell me about a situation in which a customer was so difficult that you just gave up trying (or were unable) to satisfy her.

16. Sooner or later we all have to deal with a customer who makes unreasonable demands. Think about a time when you had to handle unreasonable requests.

### Miscellaneous

17. Give me an example of a situation you handled where even your enemies would have to say that you demonstrated outstanding customer service.

18. Give me an example of when you initiated a change in a process, procedure, or operations in response to customer feedback.

## Decision Making

### Difficult Decisions

1. Tell me about one of the most difficult (or one of the best) decisions you made in the last year/six months. What made it so difficult? What process did you use to make the decision?

2. Give me an example of a time you had to make a decision where you needed to carefully consider a great deal of conflicting, as well as supporting, information, opinions, and data.

3. Give me an example of a difficult decision that you made where there were no supporting facts to guide you either way.

## Rapid Decision Making

4. Give me an example of a decision that you made rapidly and one you took more time to make.

5. Describe a time you had to make a quick decision with incomplete information.

## Bad or "Do Over" Decisions

6. Tell me about the worst on-the-job decision you've ever made.

7. We all make decisions that turn out to be mistakes. Describe a decision you made at work that you wish you could do over. What would you do differently if you could do it over again?

8. Give me an example of a time you used a contractor or consultant for something that, in hindsight, should have been done internally.

## Important Decisions

9. Give me an example of a time you had to make an important business decision that still affects you today.

10. Tell me about one of the most important decisions you have made when the information for that decision was based on the questions you asked.

## Miscellaneous

11. Tell me about a time when you took a public stance on an issue and then had to change your position.

12. Describe a time when you had to make a decision that you knew would be unpopular.

13. Give me an example of a time when you had to make a decision and policies/procedures were not in place.

14. Tell me about a situation that, if you had not acted immediately, could have turned into a major problem.

15. Give me an example of a situation when, by recognizing and considering the financial implications of a decision, you decided to do something different from what you originally planned.

16. Tell me about a time you had to defend a decision you made.

## Delegation

1. Give me an example of when you assigned an employee to make a decision or carry out a major task or responsibility.

2. Tell me about a task or project that you unsuccessfully delegated. What happened? What did you learn? How did you apply what you learned to other situations?

3. Tell me about the kinds of work assignments you give to your direct reports. What assignments do you *not* give to your direct reports?

4. Give me an example of a time that you should have delegated a task/ project, but chose not to.

5. Describe a time you had to delegate parts of a large project or assignment to some of your direct reports. How did you decide what tasks to delegate to which people? What problems occurred?

6. Give me an example of a major project or task you delegated to one of your employees. How did you monitor the project or task?

7. Give me an example of a time you did a poor job of delegating a task or project.

## Detail Orientation/Attention to Detail

1. Give me an example of a time where your attention to detail helped you avoid making a mistake.

2. Tell me about a time when you caught an error that others had missed.

3. Describe a situation where you didn't pay as close attention to the details as you should have.

4. Tell me about a time when you paid too much attention to the details and not enough to the big picture.

## Developing Direct Reports

1. Tell me about a time you had to confront and handle the negative behavior of someone who reports to you. What was the situation? What did you do? What was the outcome?

2. Tell me about a time you had to take disciplinary action with one of your direct reports. What led to that action? How did you handle it? What was the outcome?

3. Tell me about a specific developmental plan that you created and carried out with one or more of your direct reports who was not performing up to expectations. What were the components of the developmental plan? What was the timeframe? What was the outcome?

4. Tell me about a time you had to provide constructive feedback to an employee who was not meeting performance expectations. Why was the employee not meeting expectations? (*NOTE: Listen for whether the person accepts responsibility for developing employees or places the blame solely on the employees.*)

5. Describe for me the process and steps you went through to develop one of your most difficult employees. Was it successful? Why or why not?

6. Tell me about a time when you had to tell a staff member that you were dissatisfied with his work.

7. Tell me about a time you coached or mentored someone to a higher level of performance or a higher level position.

8. Tell me about a time you failed to develop someone to adequately prepare her for a task, project, or responsibility.

9. Describe what steps you have taken in your current or previous positions to define and communicate performance expectations to your employees.

10. Many of us have had to deal with a situation where an employee was a good performer for a period of time, but whose performance has started slipping. Tell me about a time you had to deal with this kind of situation.

11. Give me an example of a time you helped one of your direct reports develop or improve his (communication, negotiation, sales, etc.) skills. How did you determine that this was a developmental need?

## (Providing) Direction to Others

1. Tell me how you know what your direct reports are doing.

2. Describe your procedures for keeping track of what is going on in your department.

3. Tell me about the process you used to set goals for your department and your direct reports last year.

4. Give me an example of a time when you failed to set clear directions for one of your direct reports or your team.

5. Give me an example of a stretch goal you set for a direct report. Why was this a stretch goal? Was the direct report able to accomplish the goal? What did you do to contribute to her success?

6. Managers quite often delegate major projects to their direct reports. Tell me about a time that you did that and how you kept informed about the status of the project.

## Diversity (Valuing and Encouraging)

*Personal Focus—Adapting*

1. Tell me about a time you had to adapt to a wide variety of people by accepting or understanding their perspectives.

2. Tell me about a time you adapted your style in order to work effectively with those who were different from you.

3. Give me an example of a time when a person's cultural background affected your approach to a work situation.

### Personal Focus—Different Values/Beliefs

4. Tell me about the most difficult challenge you have faced in working cooperatively with someone who did not share your ideas, values, or beliefs. (*NOTE: Make sure you understand what the differences were.*) What was the impact on your ability to get things done? What was the impact on the other person's ability to get things done?

5. Give me an example of a time when your values and beliefs impacted your relationship with a peer, coworker, supervisor, or customer.

### Personal Focus—Work Environment

6. Tell me the steps you have taken to create a work environment where differences are valued, encouraged, and supported.

7. Describe a time you were able to make your voice heard in a predominantly opposite-sex-dominated environment.

8. Tell me about a time you took action to make someone feel comfortable in an environment that was obviously uncomfortable with his or her presence.

### Personal Focus—Miscellaneous

9. Tell me about a time you avoided forming an opinion of someone based on his outward appearance.

10. Describe a time when, in a work environment, you made an intentional effort to get to know someone from another culture.

11. Describe a time you had to separate the person from the issue when working to resolve differences.

*Encouraging Others to Value Diversity*

12. Describe a situation when you had to give feedback to someone who was not accepting of others.

13. Describe the way you handled a specific problem involving others with differing values, ideas, and beliefs in your current/previous job.

## Emotional Intelligence/Awareness

1. Give me an example of a time that your ability to notice another person's feelings or concerns enabled you to proactively address an issue.

2. Tell me about a time that your ability to appropriately use empathy turned a situation around.

3. Describe a situation where, because you were aware of the nonverbal dynamics of a person or group, you adapted your communication and turned the situation around.

4. Tell me about a time you feel you mismanaged an emotionally charged situation.

5. Give me an example of a time when, because you failed to detect a person's feelings or concerns, you—at least initially—mishandled the situation.

6. Give me an example of a time where your understanding of your own emotions—and of the triggers that set off emotional responses in you—saved you from doing or saying something in a business setting that you might have regretted.

7. Describe for me a time you were able to transform your anxiety or negative emotions into positive emotions and actions.

8. Give me an example of a time where—even though it was difficult—you were able to control and filter your emotions in a constructive way.

## Empowerment

1. Describe for me a time when you provided your direct reports with the freedom to determine their work process, within the parameters of the task/project, even though you would have preferred that they do it another way.

2. Tell me about a time you encouraged a direct report to make decisions within his area of responsibility that worked out better than you expected.

3. Give me an example of a time you encouraged a direct report to make a decision within her area of responsibility that did not work out well. What happened? What did you do? What was the final end result?

4. Tell me about a time you encouraged your direct reports to be actively involved in solving problems related to their position rather than coming to you for the answers.

5. Give me a specific example of how you have empowered your staff to make independent decisions.

6. Describe a time when, even though it was difficult, you kept quiet and let a team resolve problems on its own rather than prescribing a solution for them.

## Ethics/Values/Integrity

*Personal Issues*

1. Give me an example of a time when you were able to keep a confidence, even when you were tempted to break it or it would have been easier to break it.

2. Tell me about a specific time when you had to handle a tough problem that challenged fairness or ethical issues.

3. Give me examples of how you acted with integrity (walked your talk) in your job/work relationships.

4. Give me an example of a specific occasion in which you conformed to a policy with which you did not agree.

5. Tell me about a time when you gave the benefit of the doubt to someone and were glad that you did.

6. At times we are all faced with the situation of having to tell a customer, employee, boss, or someone else *No*, because we don't believe that *Yes*

would be the right answer—even though it would be the easy answer. Tell me about a time you faced this kind of situation.

7. Tell me about a time when you took responsibility for a mistake before anyone else even knew that you had made a mistake.

8. We are all faced with having to make a choice between two seemingly opposing things, both of which seem like the right decision. Tell me about a time you were in this situation. What did you do? Why did you choose that "right" action?

9. Discuss a time when your integrity was challenged.

10. Tell me about a time when you experienced a loss for doing what is right.

11. Tell me about a business situation when you felt honesty was inappropriate. Why?

## Handling Ethics/Values/Integrity Issues with Others

12. Tell me about a time you saw someone at work stretch or bend the rules beyond what you felt was acceptable. What did you do? Why did you take that action?

13. Give me an example of a time you had to present the unvarnished truth to someone, but were able to do it in a positive and helpful manner.

## Failure/Regret Incidents

14. We have all done things that we regretted after the fact. Give me an example of a time this happened to you. If you had it to do over again, what would you do differently?

15. Describe an occasion when you bent one of your core values or beliefs during a bad time.

16. Tell me about a time where you didn't practice what you preach.

17. Tell me about a time when you chose not to give someone the benefit of the doubt and wished, in hindsight, you had.

## Fairness to Direct Reports

1. Describe a time when you failed to treat all your direct reports equally.

2. Tell me about a time you had to have a candid discussion with one of your direct reports regarding a work-related issue.

3. Give me an example of a time you had to handle a tough employee problem that challenged your ability to remain fair to all employees.

4. Tell me about a time you gave one employee preferential treatment. Why did you do it? What was the impact?

5. Tell me about a time when you treated all your direct reports equally even though you were tempted to show preferential treatment to one or some of them.

## Flexibility/Adaptability

*Switching Gears*

1. Tell me about a time when you had to stop working on a project/idea/ assignment and start working on a completely different one. What did you do? How did that work out?

2. Give me an example of a time your tightly scheduled day was interrupted and thrown way off schedule.

3. Describe a time when you changed your behavior to fit a specific situation. (*NOTE: Make sure you find out, at minimum, what the situation was, what the specific behavior was prior to and after the change, why the behavior change was made, and whether the behavior change was appropriate in retrospect.*)

*Need to Modify or Change*

4. Tell me about a time when you changed or modified your priorities to meet another person's or group's expectations.

5. Tell me about a time when you had to change your point of view or your plans to take in account new information or a change in priorities.

6. Describe a time when you were instructed to modify or change your actions to respond to the needs of another person. Do you feel that the demand was fair? Why or why not?

7. Tell me about a time you uncovered new information that affected a decision that you had already made.

8. Tell me about a situation in which you have had to adjust to changes over which you had no control.

9. Tell me about a time when you had to adjust to another person's working style in order to complete a project/task/goal.

### Miscellaneous

10. Describe an instance when you had to think on your feet to extricate yourself from a difficult situation.

11. Describe a time when you made a major sacrifice to achieve an important goal.

### Failed/Negative Incidents

12. Give me an example of a time when you didn't bend on a policy, procedure, or operation, and later wished you had.

13. Give me an example of a time you were unwilling or unable to make the necessary sacrifice to achieve a goal.

14. Most organizations today make ongoing changes in policies and procedures. Tell me about a time you had difficulty in dealing with one of these changes. What about the change made it difficult? How did you deal with the situation?

## Functional/Technical/Job Skills

### Develop

1. Tell me about a situation in which you had to apply some newly acquired knowledge or skill. What was the knowledge or skill?

2. In your current (most recent) position, tell me how you developed an appropriate depth of knowledge and skill about the company's products/services

## Maintain

3. Tell me about the changes or issues that are being discussed or taking place in your area of expertise. How are these issues or changes affecting the way you do your job?

4. Tell me how you keep abreast of the professional/technical aspects of your position.

## Anticipate

5. Tell me about a time you anticipated the need to improve a technical/ functional skill and took action proactively.

6. Give me an example of a time you took the initiative to find out about a new or upcoming product/service change.

## Contributions to/Application in the Organization

7. Give me an example of where your understanding of your job contributed to solving a larger problem in the organization.

8. Describe a situation where your professional/technical expertise made a significant difference.

9. Tell me about a time where your industry knowledge enabled you to identify a potential problem and develop a strategy to address it. What in your knowledge base enabled you to detect the potential problem?

10. Through a real-life story, convince me that you are able to apply specific product/service knowledge to solve an internal or external problem.

11. Give me an example of how you acquired a technical skill and converted it into a practical application.

12. Tell me about your greatest success in using logic to solve a (technical/ functional/job skill) problem. Why do you think you were successful?

*Failed/Negative Incidents*

13. At some point, everyone gets in over his head. Tell me about a time this happened to you.

14. Tell me about a time you were unable to overcome a (technical/functional/ job skill) problem? Why do you think you were unsuccessful? What did you learn from that situation?

## Goal Setting/Accomplishment/Focus

*Successes*

1. Give me an example of an important goal you had to set and how you accomplished that goal.

2. Give me an example of a time when you set a goal and were able to meet or achieve it.

3. Tell me about a time when your department was going through long-term changes or working on a long-term project. What did you do to keep your staff focused?

*Failed/Negative Incidents*

4. Tell me about an important goal you failed to achieve.

5. Describe a time when you set a goal for yourself and did not achieve it because it was too high. What was the standard? Why was it too high? What were the ramifications of your failure to achieve the goal?

6. Describe a time when you set a goal for yourself that was too low.

*Processes*

7. Describe how you set your goals for last year and how you measured your work. Did you achieve your goals? If not, why not?

8. Tell me about a major project you recently finished. Specifically, how did you set the goals and monitor your progress?

9. Give me an example of a time when you used a systematic process to define your objectives even though you were not prompted or directed to do so. What type of system did you use? What payoff did you get from using the process?

*Challenges*

10. Tell me about a time you were given a goal by someone else that you believed would be impossible to attain.

11. Give me an example of a time you made a major sacrifice to achieve an important goal.

12. Tell me about a time when you were unwilling or unable to make the sacrifice necessary to achieve a goal.

13. Describe your organization's culture and how that culture made it challenging for you to achieve one of your goals.

## Hiring/Staffing

1. Give me an example of a time you were responsible for hiring and orienting a new employee. What did you do to help him learn the new job? What did you do to help him learn about the company?

2. Tell me about the best hire you ever made.

3. Tell me about the worst hire you ever made.

4. Tell me about a time you discovered raw talent within your organization and recruited that person. How did it work out?

5. Give me an example of the talents and skills that a couple of your direct reports have that you don't possess.

6. Walk me through the process you used for the last position you filled.

7. Every now and then there is a position that is hard to fill. Tell me about the last time you had to deal with that. Why was the position hard to fill? How did you overcome that obstacle?

## (Using) Humor

1. Tell me about a time you used your sense of humor to diffuse a potential problem.

2. Give me an example of a time that you did something so silly that you had to laugh at yourself.

3. Describe a situation where you used humor to ease tensions

4. Give me an example of a time where, in retrospect, if you had used your sense of humor, something at work would most likely have worked out better.

5. Tell me about a time where you used humor that backfired on you.

6. Tell me about a situation where you dealt effectively with another person's inappropriate use of humor.

7. Give me an example of a time when your ability to employ a sense of humor made you more successful than if you had not used it.

## Influencing/Persuading

1. Tell me about the best idea you ever sold to a peer, employee, or higher level management. What was your approach? Why do you think you succeeded?

2. Tell me about a time when you anticipated a problem and were able to use your influence or persuasiveness to change the direction of the situation positively.

3. Tell me how you persuaded someone to support an unpopular project or idea.

4. Describe a situation in which you were able to use persuasion to successfully convince someone to see/do things your way. (*NOTE: Make sure you find out what level the person was whom they convinced.*)

5. Tell me about a time when you used your interpersonal skills to build a network of contacts to reach goals.

6. Describe a time when you had to influence a number of different people/ groups coming from different perspectives to support you in what you wanted or needed to do. What kind of influencing techniques did you use? How were the techniques you used different from one group/person to another?

7. Give me an example of a time you had to convince others to conform to a policy, practice, or procedure you didn't believe in.

8. Tell me about a specific experience of yours that illustrates your ability to influence another person verbally. Use an example that involves _____ (e.g., changing an attitude, selling a idea, changing a process/procedure).

9. Give me an example of a time when you persuaded someone to do something that the person did not, initially, want to do.

10. Tell me about a situation where you had to persuade someone to accept your idea or proposal.

*Failed Incidents*

11. Describe a time you were unable to sell your idea to a key person.

12. Describe a situation in which you were unable to use persuasion to successfully convince someone to see/do things your way.

## Information Gathering

1. Tell me about a time where your failure to gather sufficient information resulted in your making a decision or taking an action that you probably should not have done.

2. Describe a time where your patience in gathering information paid off.

3. Tell me about the most difficult time you have had in the last couple of years gathering the information you needed for a task or project.

4. Give an example of a time where, because you didn't have enough information, you felt it was wise not to voice your opinion on something.

5. Tell me about a situation where, because you had a strong network, you were able to gather information that others were not able to secure.

## Information Sharing

1. Tell me about a time when you failed to give your team or a member of your team the information needed to do the job you asked of them.

2. Give me an example of a time you provided a direct report with information that helped her make a good decision.

3. Describe a situation where you delayed providing others with information that would have been valuable to them.

4. Give me an example of a time where you felt you did an outstanding job of sharing information with another person.

5. Keeping information confidential is very important. Describe the last time someone asked you for information that they should not have access to. What did you do?

6. Give me an example of a time when you were slow to share information with your direct reports or team members and this had a negative impact on one or more of them.

## Initiative

*Project Related*

1. Describe a significant project idea you initiated in the last year. How did you know it was needed? Was it used? How did it work?

2. Give me an example of a project where you came up with the idea and managed the process start to finish.

3. Give me an example of a project or task that you had to accomplish without sufficient information, guidelines, or direction.

4. Tell me about a project or idea—not necessarily your own—that was implemented successfully primarily because of your efforts.

*Initiating Change (Proactive)*

   5. Describe a situation where you responded proactively.

   6. Give me an example of something that you have done to make your job easier or more interesting.

   7. Describe a situation in which you recognized a potential problem as an opportunity.

*Going Above and Beyond*

   8. Give me an example of a time you went above or beyond the call of duty in order to get a job done.

   9. Describe a time where you took the initiative to act rather than waiting to be told what to do.

  10. Tell me about a time you reached out for additional responsibilities.

  11. Give me some examples of you doing more than what was expected of you in your job.

  12. Tell me about a time when you pushed yourself to do more than was necessary.

  13. Describe a time when you took the initiative to do something that needed to be done, even though it wasn't really your responsibility. What circumstances prompted you to act?

  14. We all have periods of downtime at work. Tell me about a downtime you had, why you had it, and what you did with that time.

*Failed/Negative Incidents*

  15. Give me an example of an idea you tried to sell to management that was not adopted. Why do you think it wasn't adopted? If you had it to do over again, what would you do differently?

## Interpersonal Skills/Savvy

*Building Rapport and Relationships*

   1. Describe for me a situation when you had to build and maintain a new relationship in order to accomplish a business goal.

2. Building rapport with some people can be challenging. Give an example of a time when you were able to build rapport quickly with someone in your organization, even though the situation was a difficult one.

3. Describe a time when you were able to "read" another person effectively and, as a result, were able to adjust your actions to meet this person's needs or values.

## Working with Difficult People

4. Tell me about a time when you had to deal with a (rude, sarcastic, know-it-all, gossipy, negative, uncooperative, or finger-pointing) person. How did you handle the situation? Were you able to get along? How (or why not)?

5. Tell me about a situation where you had to work closely with a difficult coworker in order for you to successfully accomplish something. Did you make it work? How (or why not)?

## Failed/Negative Incidents

6. Some people are more difficult than others to get along with. Tell me about your least successful working relationship. Why do you think it was not a successful relationship?

7. Give me an example of a situation where you misread another person and ended up making the situation worse instead of better, at least initially.

## Miscellaneous

8. Describe a project you were responsible for that required a lot of interaction with people over a long period of time.

9. Sometimes it is important to disagree with others in order to keep a mistake from being made. Tell me about a time when you were willing to disagree with another person in order to build a positive outcome. (*NOTE: Make sure you find out who the person was they disagreed with, what the outcome was, and whether the outcome was positive—or if not, what happened to keep it from being a positive outcome.*)

10. Describe for me a time when you had to—tactfully but forcefully—say things that another person or group did not want to hear.

## Learning/Knowledge Acquisition and Application

1. Tell me about a time when you had to learn something new in a short amount of time. What created the situation? What did you have to learn? How did you learn it?

2. Describe a time when you had to learn something quickly to solve a problem.

3. Give me an example of something difficult you had to learn that you did end up learning.

4. Tell me about a time you had to do an unfamiliar task.

5. Tell me about a time you needed to learn something quickly for a new task or project. How did you go about it?

6. Give me an example of a situation at one of your previous employers when others knew more than you did. How did you close the gap?

7. Walk me through the actions that you have taken to further your own professional development over the last (six months/year/five years).

8. Tell me about a job that you had that required you to learn new things.

9. We all have disappointing business experiences. Tell me about one you had and what you learned from it.

## Listening

1. Tell me about a time on your last job when you had to get a job done with only oral instructions to guide you.

2. Give me an example of a time when you were a good listener.

3. Sometimes people hear but don't listen. Tell me about a time when you misunderstood someone. Why do you think you misunderstood? How did you resolve the misunderstanding?

4. Tell me about a time where you lost your patience listening to someone who you believed did not know what she was talking about.

5. Describe a time you heard someone out, even though you initially disagreed with the person, only to change your mind in the end.

6. Give me an example of a time you had to deal with a highly emotional direct report.

7. Tell me about a time where your active listening skills really paid off for you.

8. Describe a work situation that required you to *really* listen to a person who was telling you about a personal/sensitive situation.

## Manager Relationships

1. Describe a time you were able to provide your boss with recognition for the work he performed.

2. Tell me about a time you went the "extra mile" for a boss. Why did you do it?

3. Give me an example of something that you learned from your boss that has helped you in your career.

4. Tell me about a time your boss coached you to improve your performance or to learn something new.

5. Give me some examples of the kinds of things you have talked to your boss about rather than handling them yourself.

6. Tell me about the worst boss you've had. What made her the worst boss? How were you able to work with this person?

## Managing and Measuring Work Performance

1. Tell me about the methods you use to keep informed of your employees' activities, achievements, progress toward objectives, etc.

2. Give me an example of a time you had to tell a direct report that you were dissatisfied with his work.

3. Describe your procedures for evaluating your direct reports.

4. Give me an example of a time you built a feedback loop into the work you delegated to a direct report.

5. Tell me about a major project you managed. How did you assign tasks to your direct reports? How did you monitor progress? How did you measure success along the way and in the end?

6. Give me an example of a time you had to take disciplinary action with a direct report.

7. Tell me about a time where you were not as effective as you would have liked to have been in managing an employee's or a team's work.

8. Tell me about a time you needed to implement a new (or significantly raise an existing) performance standard for your team. What was the standard? Why did you need to raise it? How did you communicate the change? How did the affected employees respond when they were told? Were people able to meet the new performance standard? If not, why not?

## Motivation

*Self-Motivation*

1. Tell me about a time you were highly motivated and your example inspired others.

2. We all get assignments we really don't want to do. Give me an example of a time that happened to you and tell me how you motivated yourself to get it done.

*Motivating Others*

3. Relate a scenario where you were responsible for motivating others. Were you able to do it? How?

4. Give me an example of a time of low morale where you were able to motivate another person or group to achieve something that they weren't really motivated to achieve.

5. Tell me about a time when you provided your direct reports or a team with the things they needed to motivate themselves to an extraordinary accomplishment.

6. Tell me about a time when you were able to give an employee what she needed to maintain or regain her motivation.

7. Tell me about a time you had to handle a tough morale problem.

## Negotiation

1. Tell me about a time when you gained acceptance of an idea or project from your boss. How did you get this acceptance?

2. Give me an example of an approach you used to sell an idea to an employee, peer, or someone higher in management.

3. Describe for me a situation where two individuals or parties were at odds, and you helped negotiate a win-win solution.

4. Tell me about a time you needed to get cooperation from someone in another department for you to be successful on a task or project.

5. Tell me about the most important negotiation you have handled in the last couple of years.

6. Tell me about a time that you were successful in a negotiation because you backed off of something that was part of the negotiation.

7. Tell me about a time you were unsuccessful in a negotiation because you chose not to back off of something that was part of the negotiation.

8. Give me an example of a time you were unhappy with the results of a negotiation you were involved in.

9. Tell me about a time you won (lost) an important contract.

## Organization

1. Tell me about a time you had to handle multiple responsibilities. How did you organize the work you needed to do?

2. Give me some examples of how you determine priorities in scheduling your time.

3. With fax machines, e-mail, and other technology speeding up processes, time seems to be something we are always running low on. Describe some things you have done to organize your work in the past to meet the various time demands.

4. Tell me about a time you were particularly effective in prioritizing tasks and completing a project on schedule.

5. Tell me about one of your best accomplishments, including where the assignment came from, your plans in carrying it out, how you eventually did carry it out, and any obstacles you overcame.

6. Give me an example of a time when you had to juggle several important activities and projects in a limited amount of time. Did you stay on top of all of them? How?

7. Describe how you have improved the organization of a system, process, or task in your current position.

8. Tell me about a time you had multiple tasks or projects given to you at the same time and how you decided what to do when.

9. Tell me about a time you got bogged down in the details of a project.

10. Tell me about the last time you missed a deadline because you were not well organized.

## Organizational Agility/Awareness

*Positive Examples*

1. Tell me about a time when you needed to accomplish something through an informal network.

2. Describe a time where your ability to understand an organization's culture helped you develop the relationships and partnerships you needed to accomplish something that had to be done.

3. Tell me about the organizational climate at your current (or most recent) employer and give me an example of how that climate made it difficult for you to successfully accomplish a goal or project.

4. Give me an example of a time when your ability to read an organization's culture enabled you to be successful at something.

5. Tell me about a time you were able to accomplish something that was important to you through the use of your informal network.

## Failed/Negative Examples

6. Give me an example of a time when, if you had taken more time to understand how your organization worked, you might have been more successful.

7. Tell me about a time when you misread an organization's culture.

8. Give me an example of a time where, had you understood the reasoning behind a key policy, practice, or procedure, you would have done something differently.

# Partnering (Internal/External)

1. Describe for me a time you developed and maintained (or strengthened) a relationship with a person or group *inside* your organization. Why did you develop the relationship? How did you develop it? What did you do to maintain/strengthen it?

2. Give me an example of a time you developed and maintained (or strengthened) a relationship with a person or group *outside* the organization. Why did you develop the relationship? How did you develop it? What did you do to maintain/strengthen it?

3. Most things we do have an impact on others—whether we realize it or not. Tell me about a time you realized that what you would be working on could

have a far-reaching impact, and you sought out relevant/appropriate people to gather their concerns and perspective before you proceeded with the task.

4. Tell me about a time you got involved in a cross-functional activity simply to develop a better working relationship with those involved in the activity.

5. Give me an example of when you wish you would have spent some time looking for common ground with stakeholders before you took a particular action.

6. Describe for me a time when you might have been more successful at something had you taken the time to clarify the expectations in a working relationship.

7. Tell me about a time that you failed to put in the required effort to maintain an internal or external working relationship.

## Patience

1. Tell me about a time where you lost your patience listening to someone who you believed did not know what he was talking about.

2. Give me an example of a time where you felt that a process was getting in your way of getting something done.

3. Describe a process or procedure that guides your actions, but for which you have little patience.

4. Tell me about a time when you failed to gather sufficient information before acting.

5. Give me an example of a time that you misjudged a person or data.

6. Give me an example of a specific occasion when you conformed to a policy with which you did not agree. Why did you comply? What would have been the consequences of noncompliance?

7. Tell me about the biggest error in judgment you made in your current position. Why did you make the error? How did you correct it?

## Peer Relations

1. Describe a time you were able to provide a peer or higher-level management person with recognition for the work she performed.

2. Give me an example of a time where you had a disagreement with one of your peers, but were able to find common ground and solve the problem.

3. Tell me about a time you needed to gain the trust and support of one of your peers in order to be successful on something.

4. Describe a time you had to give candid feedback to one of your peers.

5. Give me an example of a time you were a team player in a project with your peers.

6. Tell me about a time you had to deal with a coworker who was very upset.

## Perseverance

*General*

1. Tell me about a time when you stayed with an idea or project for longer than anyone expected you to.

2. Tell me about some of the obstacles you have had to overcome to reach your present position.

3. Tell me about a time when you had to finish a job even though everyone else had given up.

4. Tell me about a time you encountered significant resistance or a major setback on a project you were working on, but managed to work through it anyway.

5. Describe a time when you were asked to complete a difficult task or project where the odds were against you. Were you successful? What did you learn from the experience?

6. All jobs have unpleasant tasks. Tell me about the most unpleasant tasks you were required to do at work. Why or why weren't you successful in getting it done?

7. Tell me about a really tough day that you had recently and what you did to get through it.

8. Describe a situation when you had to get a job done in spite of an unforeseen problem.

9. Describe your most challenging project or situation and how you overcame the obstacles.

### Failed/Negative Incidents

10. Tell me about a time when you were unable initially to sell an idea to your boss, an employee, or a peer, and so you tried again. What did you do differently the second or third time?

11. Give me an example of a time that you gave up on something before you finished. Why did you give up?

12. Give me an example of a time when you tried to accomplish something and failed. Why did you fail? If you had it to do over again, what would you do differently?

## Personal Growth and Development

### Self-Awareness and Reflection

1. Think about a time when setting a positive example had a highly beneficial impact on people you worked with. How did you determine that a strong example was needed? What did you do? What was the effect on the people?

2. Tell me the one thing about you as an employee that you hope your current or last boss doesn't tell me during a reference call.

3. Tell me about a time when you were not pleased with (or were disappointed in) your performance. What did you do about it?

4. Tell me about a time when one of your weaknesses got the better of you.

5. Give me an example of a time that you used one of your strengths to help another person or team succeed.

6. Describe a work situation that brought out the worst in you. Why did it bring out the worst in you? What did you learn?

7. Tell me about something you did in your (last/current) position of which you are particularly proud.

## Lessons Learned

8. Give me an example of a time that you failed at something (or made a mistake) and learned. What did you learn? How did you apply that learning?

9. Describe for me your biggest error in judgment or failure in your (current or last) position. Why did you make it? How did you correct the problem?

10. Tell me about a time when you were asked to complete a difficult assignment even though the odds were against you. What did you learn from that experience?

11. Give me an example of a disappointment you had to handle in the past year. How did you cope with it?

## Self-Improvement

12. We all have weaknesses that can interfere with our success. Tell me about one of yours and how you overcame it to be successful on a specific task or project.

13. Give me an example of something that you have done in the past to improve yourself.

14. Describe a situation in which you received constructive feedback about your work. What was the feedback about? What was your assessment of the feedback? What did you do with the information you received? What changes did you make?

## Perspective

1. Tell me about a time where your ability to (think globally/broadly/strategically, or look at the big picture) stopped you or someone else from doing something that would have been a mistake.

2. Tell me about a time you had tunnel vision when looking at a project, issue, or problem.

3. Give me an example of a time where you were able to pose a variety of future scenarios to ensure that the proper course of action was taken.

4. Describe a time for me when you were able to solve a business problem or challenge by applying something that you learned through a personal or business interest of yours.

5. Tell me about a time when your ability to explore "what if . . ." scenarios enabled you to address a significant/major problem from occurring.

## Planning/Priority Setting

*General*

1. Give me an example of a change you saw coming and how you planned for that change.

2. Give me an example of an important goal that you had set for your team and the team's success in reaching it.

3. Give me an example of a time you had a lot of tasks put on your plate all at once. How did you decide what tasks to do and when to do them?

4. Tell me about a big project you had to plan for work.

5. Tell me about your current top priorities. How did you determine that they should be your top priorities?

6. Give me an example of a time when you were effective in doing away with the "constant emergencies" and "surprises" in your work environment.

7. Tell me about a time when you had too many things to do and you were required to prioritize your tasks.

8. Give me an example of a time when your schedule was suddenly interrupted and your plans for the day completely changed.

9. Think about the assignments you completed over the past few months. Tell me about the one that required the greatest amount of effort with regard to planning and organizing.

*Failed/Negative Incidents*

10. Describe a time when your plans didn't work out. What did you do to recover?

11. Give me a specific example of a time when you did not meet a deadline. How did you handle this?

12. Describe a time when your plan didn't work out. Why didn't it work? What did you do to recover? Were you successful then? If you had to do it over again, what would you do differently? What did you learn from this? How have you applied what you learned?

## Political Awareness/Savvy

1. Describe a politically sensitive situation that you were in and how you handled it.

2. Tell me about a time that you consciously chose not to play corporate politics.

3. Give me an example of a complex political situation you were able to handle effectively and quietly, which, had you not handled it well, could have blown up.

4. Describe a time when you agreed to implement someone else's idea over your own. How did you approach the situation? How did you feel about it? Was it a successful implementation? Why/why not?

5. Describe a time when you were able to anticipate a land mine and plan your upcoming actions accordingly.

6. Tell me about a time your willingness to play politics made you successful.

7. Describe a time when politics at work affected your job. How did you handle the situation? Were you successful?

8. Give me an example of a time you used your political savvy to push something through for approval.

*Failures/Learning from Failures*

9. Tell me about a time that you unknowingly stepped on a political landmine. What contributed to this misstep? Was it resolved effectively? How?

10. Tell me about a time where you were unable to successfully navigate through a political situation.

11. Describe an instance when you had to think on your feet to extricate yourself from a difficult situation.

## Presentation Skills

1. Tell me about a presentation you made to a large audience. What was the purpose? How did you prepare it?

2. Give me an example of a presentation you did for a small group that resulted in the group agreeing to do what you wanted.

3. Describe a situation where, after a presentation, you were faced with a hostile questioner. What did you do? What were the results?

4. Give me an example of a time when a presentation you were making wasn't working and you were able to switch tactics to make it work. How did you know the presentation wasn't working?

5. Tell me about an oral presentation you made to a group within the last year. What was the most difficult aspect of the presentation?

6. Describe the most creative oral presentation you have had to make.

7. Describe the most significant presentation you have had to complete.

8. Tell me about a time you had to use your presentation skills to influence someone's opinion.

## Problem Solving

*Gathering/Analyzing/Using Facts and Information*

1. Describe a problem situation where you had to seek out relevant information, define key issues, and decide on which steps to take to get the desired results.

2. Give me an example of a time when you used your fact-finding skills to solve a problem.

3. Tell me about a situation where the analysis that you performed was incorrect. If you had it to do over again, what would you do differently?

4. Tell me about a project that best demonstrates your analytical abilities.

## Catching Problems Early

5. We can sometimes identify a small problem and fix it before it becomes a major problem. Give me an example of how you have done this.

6. Give me an example of a time you identified a potential problem and resolved the situation before it became serious.

7. Describe a time you failed to anticipate a potential problem and develop preventative measures.

## Miscellaneous

8. Give me an example of the most creative solution to a difficult problem you have ever come up with.

9. Tell me about a time you helped resolve a group problem. What caused the problem?

10. Tell me about the most difficult problem you've ever had to solve. What steps did you take to tackle it?

11. Solving a problem often necessitates evaluation of alternate solutions. Give me an example of a time when you actively defined several solutions to a single problem. *(NOTE: Make sure they talk about the tools used—e.g., research, brainstorming—as well as how and why they used the tools.)*

12. Give me a specific example of a time when you used good judgment and logic in solving a problem.

13. Tell me about a stubborn or recurring problem you are facing in your current position. What have you done to solve it?

14. Tell me about a time you had to solve a problem with no rules, guidelines, or policies in place to guide you.

15. We all have particular problems we enjoy/dislike solving. Tell me about a problem that you enjoyed solving (or disliked having to solve). What, in particular, do you enjoy/dislike about solving this kind of problem?

16. Tell me about a difficult problem you solved that had a significant positive impact on all or part of the organization.

## Failed/Negative Incidents

17. Tell me about a problem that got out of control before you discovered it and began working on a solution.

18. Tell me about a time you missed an obvious solution to a problem.

# Process Management

1. Tell me the process you used last year (or this year) to set your department goals. Were the goals accomplished?

2. Tell me about your system for controlling errors in your work.

3. Walk me through a recent project or assignment you completed and tell me the process you used to ensure it was complete and accurate.

4. Give me an example of a situation where you improved a work process.

5. Tell me about a time when you took a complicated, technical process and explained it to people who were not familiar with the process.

6. Tell me about a significant project that you managed, focusing on how you made sure that everything was getting done correctly and properly.

7. Give me an example of a time you saw an opportunity to integrate two or more processes or procedures to make a more efficient and effective single process or procedure.

8. Tell me about a situation where you found a way to get the job done faster and better at a lower cost.

## Resource Management

1. We all have more on our plate than we have time to get done. Tell me about a time where your ability to accurately scope out time requirements for tasks and projects made you successful.

2. Tell me about a time where you prepared a budget larger than any you had ever done before. Did you meet the budget? What was the variance? Did the budget need to be altered (if so, how and why)?

3. Describe a time you had to manage a project where the acquisition, storage, and use of materials were critical factors (e.g., the product had a short shelf life).

4. Give me an example of a time where you underestimated a resource you needed to get a task or project done, but managed to overcome the shortage and be successful.

5. Tell me about a time where you were off-target on assessing the human resources you needed for a project. Why were you off-target?

6. Describe a time you had to deal with a particularly difficult resource management issue regarding people/material/assets.

7. We have all faced situations where the resources we needed to be successful were not within our span of control. Tell me about a project or goal where this was true for you.

8. Sometimes the only way people or departments can accomplish their individual goals is to form a partnership. Tell me about a time where, had you not partnered, your individual goals might not have been achieved.

## (Showing) Respect

1. Tell me about a time when you had to resolve a difference of opinion with a coworker/customer/supervisor. How do you feel you showed respect for that person?

2. Tell me about a time when you needed to give feedback to an employee with emotional or sensitive problems.

3. Describe the way you handled a specific problem involving others with differing values, ideas, and beliefs in your current/previous job.

4. Describe a work situation that required you to really listen to and display compassion for a coworker/employee who was telling you about a personal or sensitive issue.

5. Give me an example of a time when you disagreed with the views of your direct reports.

6. Tell me about a time you had to handle a highly emotional person.

7. Describe for me a time when you saw a situation very differently from someone else and disagreed strongly with him, but still respected his viewpoint.

## Results Orientation

1. Give me an example of an important goal you have had and about your success in achieving it.

2. Describe a time when, against all odds, you were able to get a project or task completed within the defined parameters.

3. Tell me about a time when you were asked to complete a difficult assignment and the odds were against you. What did you learn from the experience?

4. Tell me about a time you had to pay close attention to the tiny details in order to be successful.

5. Being successful takes more than luck—it also takes hard work. Tell me about a time when you had to work very hard and make personal sacrifices to help your organization/department/team reach its goals.

### Failed/Negative Incidents

6. Give me an example of a time you were unable to complete a project on time.

7. Tell me about a time where you did not achieve the results you should have had or in the required timeframe.

8. Describe a situation where, due to time and resource constraints, you submitted a report or completed a project where the quality was compromised.

## Risk Taking

1. Tell me about a time where, with an internal or external customer, you had to try something you've never done before.

2. Give me an example of a time you felt that it was necessary or appropriate to circumvent company policy to meet a customer's needs.

3. Describe for me the riskiest business decision you have ever made. Why did you make the decision? Were you successful and why or why not?

4. Describe a work-related risk you took that, in hindsight, you wish you had not taken.

5. Tell me about a time when you created a new process or program that was considered risky. What was the situation and what did you do?

6. Give me an example of a time when there was a decision to be made and procedures or policies were not in place. What was the outcome?

7. Tell me about the greatest business risk you have taken.

8. Tell me about a time you had a chance to take a risk, but decided that the risk was too high.

9. Tell me about a time you took a risk and failed.

## Safety in the Workplace

1. In many situations, employees are required to wear protective equipment, and may find it uncomfortable, cumbersome, or inconvenient to wear. Tell me about a time this was true for you. (*NOTE: Make sure you find out what the equipment was, why the person did or didn't wear the equipment, and the factors that contributed to the decision.*)

2. Safety is not a one-person job. Give me an example of a time you were able to improve safety only because you chose to involve others in making the improvement.

3. Tell me about the most challenging safety issue you have had to deal with. What, specifically, made it challenging?

4. Describe a time when you identified a potential safety issue and addressed it before a problem occurred.

5. Tell me about a way you have made your workplace a safer place for people to work.

## Self-Improvement, Learning, and Development

*Positive Incidents*

1. Tell me about a time when you had to learn something new or difficult in a short amount of time. What created the situation? What did you have to learn? How did you learn it?

2. Tell me about a time you had to do an unfamiliar task.

3. Give me an example of something that you have done in the past to improve yourself.

4. Give me an example of a situation when others knew more than you did. How did you close the gap?

5. Tell me about something you did in your (last/current) position of which you are particularly proud.

6. Tell me about something specific you did to develop yourself that distinguished you from others.

7. Give me an example of a time that you used one of your strengths to help another person or team succeed.

*Learning from Failure*

8. Describe a time when you were not very satisfied or pleased with your performance. What did you do about it?

9. Tell me about a time when you were able to treat a negative experience as a learning opportunity.

10. Tell me about a work-related decision you made or a situation you handled where, if you had it to do over again, you would do something different.

11. Describe a work situation that brought out the worst in you. Why did it bring out the worst in you? What did you learn?

12. Tell me about a time when one of your weaknesses got the better of you.

13. Give me an example of a time that you failed at something and learned. What did you learn? How did you apply that learning? How did it change your work style or approach?

14. Tell me about a time you received constructive feedback from a boss or coworker that you took to heart and did something about.

15. We all have weaknesses that can interfere with our success. Tell me about one of yours and how you overcame it to be successful on a specific task or project.

16. Tell me the one thing about you as an employee that you hope your current/last boss doesn't tell me during a reference call.

17. Describe for me a time when you were disappointed in your performance.

## Stewardship/Corporate Citizenship

1. Tell me about a collaborative effort you headed (were involved in) between your organization and the community.

2. Give me an example of how your understanding of a community issue helped you address a business problem, issue, or concern.

3. Describe for me something you were involved with in the community through which both the community and businesses located in the community benefited.

4. Tell me about a way that you have championed the concept of corporate citizenship/stewardship within your team/department/organization.

## Strategic Planning/Thinking

1. Tell me about a time when your industry knowledge alerted you to an upcoming challenge or opportunity, and where you were able to develop a proactive strategy to deal with it.

2. Give me an example of a strategy you developed to achieve a long- or short-term business need, goal, or objective.

3. Give me an example of a time where, by using your understanding of the strengths and weaknesses of your competitors, you were able to gain a competitive advantage in the marketplace.

4. Tell me about a strategic initiative or opportunity you identified and pursued.

5. Give me an example of a time you failed to align the strategic priorities of your department/team with the strategic priorities of the organization.

6. Tell me about a time where your ability to keep your eyes on the future proved to be a benefit to your organization/department/team.

## Stress Management

1. Tell me about a time you were faced with stressors at work that tested your coping skills.

2. Give me an example of a time you had to juggle a number of projects and priorities. What were they? How did you manage to juggle them?

3. Describe for me a time when your team was under a fair amount of stress. What did you do to help them through this? Were you successful?

4. Tell me about a time you did not handle a stressful situation well.

5. Tell me about a time a deadline was moved up on you and how you handled that. Did you accomplish the task on time? How (or why not)?

6. There are times we each feel overwhelmed with a task or project. Tell me about a time this happened to you.

7. Describe a situation or time when someone or something really got under your skin.

8. Tell me about a project that required you to work well under pressure.

## Systems Management

1. Tell me about a time where your understanding of a (social/organizational/technological) system helped you be more successful than you would have been otherwise.

2. Give me an example of a time when you picked up on a business or industry trend or change and made appropriate changes within your company/department/team to respond to or take advantage of the opportunity.

3. Describe a time where, had you been able to predict a business/industry occurrence, you would have been able to make adjustments so that your company/department/team did not suffer from it.

4. Tell me about a system you designed or improved. Why did you do it? What benefit resulted? Who was impacted by the design/improvement? How did they react?

## Systems Thinking

1. Give me an example when your ability to look at problems and issues from a big picture approach served you well.

2. Tell me about the most significant project you have worked on in which it was crucial to keep track of details while still managing the "big picture." How did you make sure the work got done? How did you keep focused on the overall goal while still managing all of the specific parts?

3. Tell me about a time when you failed to look at a problem or issue from a big picture perspective and paid the price for that.

4. Describe for me a time when your ability to find relationships between things inside and/or outside the organization helped you be more effective.

5. Give me an example of a time you solved a problem in ways that addressed total system needs rather than just your immediate situation.

## Taking Charge

1. Tell me about a time when you had to convince your team to do something they didn't want to do. How did you do it?

2. Give me an example of when your staff reached a goal because they willingly followed your suggestions.

3. Give me a specific example of something you did that helped build enthusiasm in your staff.

4. Describe a time when you utilized your leadership ability to gain support for something that was initially strongly opposed by others.

5. Tell me about a time you found it necessary to tactfully, but forcefully, say things that others did not want to hear.

6. Tell me about a time when you had to take charge and start the ball rolling to get a job done. What were the ramifications if the job didn't get done? What did you do? How did it turn out?

7. Describe for me the most unpopular stand you have taken in your job.

## Teamwork (Encouraging and Building)

*Getting Groups/Individuals to Cooperate*

1. Describe a time you led a team of people who didn't always see eye to eye. What did you do? Why did you choose to do that? How did it work out?

2. Tell me about a time you were able to gain commitment from others to really work as a team.

3. Provide an example of a time when it was critical that you establish an effective working relationship with an individual or group outside your department to complete an assignment or deliver a service.

4. Tell me about a time you needed to get two groups or people to work together effectively, who historically had never done so.

5. Give me an example of a time that your leadership transformed a group of people into an effective, healthy, productive team.

6. Tell me about a time you led a team that had one or more unproductive/ negative members. How did you find out about the unproductive member? What did you do? Why did you choose to do that? How did it work out?

7. Give me an example of a time where you needed to get people who have very different work styles to work cooperatively on a project. Were you successful? Why/why not?

8. Describe a time when you had to have coworkers with different work styles or ideas work together on a project. What, specifically, did you do to pull them together?

## Team/Team Member Strengths

9. Tell me about a time you recognized a team member for having made a valuable contribution to the team.

10. Tell me about a time where, if it hadn't been for teamwork, your goal might not have been achieved.

## Miscellaneous

11. Describe a time when you were able to build team spirit in an environment of low morale.

12. Tell me about a time you needed to lead an intact, project, or ad hoc team toward a goal that you, personally, did not completely support or believe in.

13. Give me an example of a time you successfully built a project team from scratch. What was the project? How did you go about selecting team members? How did you get these individuals to work as a team? What was the hardest part of getting them to work as a team? Was the team successful on the project?

14. Tell me about a time when you were able to provide your team with recognition for the work they performed.

*Failed/Negative Incidents*

15. Give me an example of a time when you were less successful as a team leader than you would like to have been.

16. Tell me about a time where, because you didn't effectively build your team, you were not able to accomplish a task/project within specifications. What happened? What did you learn? What would you do differently if you had it to do over again?

## Teamwork (Working as a Team Player)

*Problems Among/with Fellow Team Members*

1. Tell me about a time you worked as a team member on a team that had one or more unproductive members. What did you do? Why did you choose to do that? How did it work out?

2. Give me an example of a time when others with whom you were working on a project disagreed with your idea.

3. Describe a time when one of the members on your team did not complete (or wasn't doing) her fair share of the work.

4. Tell me about a time when you helped others compromise for the good of the team. What was your role? What steps did you take?

5. Tell me about a time when you were part of a team that did not get along or did not work well together. What happened?

6. We've all been part of a work team or project team where there is one person who just rubs us the wrong way. Tell me about a time this happened to you. What did you do?

*Positive Incidents*

7. Give me an example of when you worked cooperatively as a team member to accomplish an important goal. What was the goal or objective? What was your role in achieving this objective? To what extent did you interact with others on this project?

8. Give me an example of a time where you were willing to compromise on something relatively important to you in order for the team you were a member of to proceed with a project.

9. Tell me about a time you were recognized and rewarded for being a valuable team member.

*Failures/Disappointments*

10. Give me an example of a time when you were not an effective team member.

11. Describe a team experience you found disappointing. What, specifically, made it disappointing. What could you have done to change it from a disappointing to rewarding experience?

## Technology Management/Utilization

1. Give me an example of a time when you were responsible for selecting a new or improved technology.

2. Tell me about a time when you misinterpreted the intent or use of a piece of equipment.

3. Describe a time when you applied a new piece of technology to an existing task or project. What benefits resulted from the technological application? How did you determine there would be a benefit?

4. Give me an example of a time where you prevented, identified, or solved a problem with a piece of equipment.

5. Tell me about a time you applied technology to improve a service, process, or productivity.

## Time Management

1. Tell me about a time you achieved a great deal in a short amount of time.

2. Give me an example of a time you were unable to complete a project on schedule despite your best efforts.

3. Tell me about a time you had to complete multiple tasks/projects in a tight timeframe.

4. Tell me about a time when you wasted the time of someone else working on something that was unimportant to the organization, but important to you.

5. Give me an example of a time that your priorities were changed quickly. What did you do? What was the result?

6. By way of example, convince me that you can get more done in less time than others.

## Trust

1. Tell me about a time you mistrusted another employee, resulting in tension between the two of you. What did you do to improve the relationship? Where you successful in improving it?

2. Give me an example of a time you failed to keep your boss informed of your actions or progress on a task or project.

3. Give me an example of a time that you failed to walk-the-talk at work.

4. Tell me about a time you had to give the benefit of the doubt to someone at work.

5. Tell me about a time when your trustworthiness was challenged. How did you react/respond?

6. Tell me how you have developed trust and loyalty between you and your direct reports.

7. Describe a situation where you distrusted a coworker/supervisor, resulting in tension between you. What steps did you take to improve the relationship?

8. Trust requires personal accountability. Tell me about a time when you chose to trust someone.

## Understanding Others

1. Give me an example to convince me that you understand why groups do what they do.

2. Tell me about a time you had to motivate a group of people.

3. Describe a time when your ability to pick up on the intentions or needs of a group resulted in you changing your course of action.

4. Tell me about a time where your understanding of what a group valued helped you work effectively with them.

5. Give me an example of a time when you were able to foresee an inappropriate course of action a team was moving and help steer them in the right direction.

6. Tell me about a time you gave someone or a group what they needed even though they didn't yet know it was needed.

## Vision and Purpose

1. Tell me about a time where your vision of the future was so inspiring that you were able to convert nay-sayers into followers.

2. Tell me about a time you lost track of the vision/mission/purpose of your team/department/organization and it turned out to have repercussions.

3. Describe a time you established a vision for your department/unit. What process was used? Were others involved in setting the vision and, if so, how? How did the vision contribute to the functioning of the department/unit?

4. Tell me about the relationship of your goals in your current position to the organization as a whole.

5. Tell me about a time when you anticipated the future and made changes to meet these future needs. Did the anticipated future occur?

CHAPTER 4

# Probing or Follow-Up Questions

**Sometimes, candidates will not provide** complete STAR (Situation, Task, Action, Results) responses to a question; other times you may simply want to get more information or clarification beyond what the candidate provided. There are a number of reasons that candidates don't give complete STAR responses. For example, candidates may be:

- Unfamiliar and therefore uncomfortable with behavioral/competency interviewing
- Trying to avoid an area or issue
- In the habit of speaking in generalities
- Reluctant to talk, for some specific reason
- Inherently shy

Whatever the reason, asking probing or follow-up questions allows you to get sufficient information on each situation to enable you to make an accurate assessment of the candidate's competency level. Probing questions are beneficial in at least four different ways:

1. *Probing questions enable you to focus the candidate on providing real-world examples.* Since many candidates are not familiar with CBBI and/or comfortable answering CBBI questions, they tend to fall back on comfortable behaviors: answering the question as if

you posed a situational question (e.g., "What would you do if . . ."). Probing questions can be used to prompt the candidate to provide you with a specific example. The conversation, in this situation, may sound something like the following:

> *Interviewer*: "We've all had to deal with unhappy customers from time to time. Tell me how you handled your most difficult customer."
>
> *Candidate*: "The process I find to be the most successful in dealing with difficult customers is to first . . ."
>
> *Interviewer*: "How often would you say you have to use this process?"
>
> *Candidate*: "Probably about once a week."
>
> *Interviewer*: "Tell me about the most difficult customer you've dealt with in the last couple of months."
>
> *Candidate*: "Well, that would have to be the call I got from . . ."

2. *Probing questions provide a means for gathering additional information or clarification on the situation the candidate related.* We have all personally been in the situation when talking casually with friends where we are telling a story and forget some of the details or make assumptions that the people who are listening know certain things. The same thing happens during interviews. Candidates are nervous and will sometimes forget to provide some details. As a result, the story that you are hearing sounds incomplete or doesn't make sense. Follow-up questions help fill in the gaps in the story. For example, "You mentioned someone named Ashley. How does this person fit into the situation?"

3. *When you are concerned about the authenticity of a candidate's story, probing questions provide a method for uncovering any inconsistencies.* Probing or follow-up questions will test for consistency and inconsistency. They help you determine whether the candidate actually exhibited the desired behavior in that particular situation.

For example, a candidate may relate a story in answer to a question and constantly say something like:

"First, we . . ."

"When we found out, we . . ."

"So, we had to make adjustments . . ."

"Our goal at that point was to . . ."

These kinds of phrases should raise a red flag: Exactly who is "we"? The candidate could be using "we" for a number of reasons, including wanting to:

- Show modesty by not taking credit
- Convey that it truly was a team effort and everyone contributed equally
- Make it sound like he had a larger role than he actually did
- Take credit for something that others on the team actually did.

4. *Probing questions enable you to uncover "nice to have" competencies.* Sometimes a candidate will make a comment while relating a situation that you would like to explore further. While it may only be indirectly related to the competency question, it could reveal that the candidate has "nice to have" competencies that could put her ahead of others, all else being equal.

Imagine that Position Y has a competency of "leading teams." When responding to the behavioral question on this point, the candidate mentions a diversity issue. You work in an organization that highly values diversity—and has a very diverse workforce. Your probing question may be something like, "You said that when you were put in charge of that project team, there were some underlying tensions you thought might be related to the diversity of the group. Tell me more about how you came to that conclusion and what you did."

Whatever your reason for using probing questions, remember that they need to be nonthreatening, nonjudgmental, and should only be used as a tool to uncover all the information you need to make a solid, valid assessment of the candidate's competency level.

Some probing or follow-up questions are:

- Who did _____?
- Specifically, what did you do (what was your role)?
- What did you say?
- What steps/actions did you take?
- I'm not sure I understand about _____. Would you tell me more about it?
- You said _____. I'm not sure I understand exactly what you mean. Could you expand on that some more?
- What happened after that?
- What were your specific duties or responsibilities?
- What was your specific contribution to the task or project?
- What did you say?
- How did the other person respond?
- How did he react?
- How did you react?
- How did you feel when _____?
- What was your role?
- What did you actually do?
- What did you actually say?
- What was the result?
- Who else was involved?
- What other options did you consider?
- What happened after _____?
- Why did you decide to do that?

- What was your logic/reasoning in doing _____?
- Tell me more about your interaction with (that person).
- What happened before _____?
- How did you deal with _____? (Followed by): Was that effective?
- You said _____. Tell me more about that.
- Exactly how were you able to _____?
- What did you think when that happened?
- What were you thinking when _____?
- How did you deal with that?
- How did you know there was a problem?
- Why did that happen?
- What was your reaction?
- How did the other person respond?
- How do you think other people felt about what you did?
- How did everything turn out in the end?
- What was the end result?
- What did you learn from the situation that you've used?
- Is there anything else I should know about that situation?
- Were you happy/satisfied with that outcome? Why (or why not)?
- What do you wish you had done differently?
- What did you learn from that?
- What were the obstacles you faced and how did you overcome them?
- What were you thinking at that point?
- How did you prepare for that?
- Can you be more specific about _____?
- Can you give me an example of that?
- What was going through your mind when you _____?
- If you could do it over again, what would you do differently and why?

There are a couple of things to keep in mind when asking prob-ing questions. First, don't ask questions where the answer is obvi-ous (otherwise known as "duh" questions). For example, "I imagine your next step in the process would be X. Am I right?" I can guarantee you that you are going to be right about 99 percent of the time. It's the rare applicant who will say, "No, my next step would be Z."

Second, avoid probing questions that could mislead, trick, or otherwise trap the applicant. This would include giving the impres-sion you would do something that you wouldn't. For example, "I sometimes wonder if the only way to deal with a screaming cus-tomer is to just hang up on them. Do you think a customer who screams at you is a customer whom you really want to work that hard to maintain?"

Finally, it never hurts to remind ourselves that we should never ask a probing—or any other type of question—that could be con-sidered discriminatory, for legal as well as ethical reasons. Also, under any circumstance, do not ask any questions that are not completely job-related.

# Initial Telephone Screening Interview

**While it may not be necessary** to conduct an initial telephone screening interview for every position, telephone screening interviews are becoming more commonplace. Companies are finding that telephone screening interviews are extremely cost- and time-effective because it helps them determine whether a candidate possesses the basic qualifications for the position—beyond those that appear on the résumé. These basic qualifications might include a specific experience or knowledge base (such as dealing with the federal government), a willingness to travel extensively, salary requirements, other "must haves," or *bona fide* occupational qualifications (BFOQs).

In short, the telephone screening interview decreases the likelihood that you will bring candidates in for face-to-face interviews who look good on paper but don't have the basic requirements for the position.

An initial telephone screening interview may be applicable when:

1. There are basic technical skills required for the position that tend not to be readily apparent on résumés.

2. There are specific and essential abilities/capabilities the candidate must possess, such as the ability to lift fifty pounds eight to ten times a day.

3. You are concerned that candidates may be looking for a higher salary than what the position pays.

4. There are specific position requirements that the candidate must be amenable to, such as a willingness to relocate or to travel a certain percentage of the time.

5. There is a need to learn more about the candidate's experience/skill/knowledge beyond those listed on the résumé, without which he would not be a viable candidate.

If you decide that an initial telephone screening interview would be of value, you need to approach it with the same forethought and consideration as you would a face-to-face interview. Remember that you are representing the company when you conduct the screening interview and that the same legal guidelines apply as in conducting a face-to-face interview. This would include calling the candidate in advance to schedule a mutually convenient time and date for the interview. You might also let the candidate know, at that point, that you will be conducting a CBBI telephone screening interview. The advantage of doing this is that the candidate is more likely to research CBBI and be prepared to answer these types of questions.

In addition to these considerations, there are five guidelines to conducting a successful telephone screening interview:

1. Develop and use a telephone screening interview form.

2. Keep the interview short.

3. Don't hold an in-depth discussion of the job requirements during the interview.

4. Conduct a legal interview.

5. Use the proper equipment.

Let's look at each of these individually.

## 1. Developing and Using a Telephone Screening Form

There is no magic number of questions to ask during a telephone screening interview, nor is there a required form (other than what your organization might require). While you can use a generic, one-form-fits-all-positions telephone screening form, it will probably not serve you well. For example, I would hope that the basic requirements that would get a computer programmer's foot in the door for an interview would be different from those that would justify a face-to-face interview with a brain surgeon.

For a specific position, however, you should use the same form with every candidate you contact for a telephone screening interview. This ensures not only that you get the same information from all potential candidates—and that you get all the information you need—but that you do it in a legally appropriate and consistent manner.

The best approach is to come up with a position-specific telephone interview form. The good news is that once you develop the form, you will not have to redo it again until the basic requirements for the position change. Then, it is simply a matter of making any necessary adjustments on the form, rather than rebuilding from scratch.

To determine what needs to be on the telephone screening interview form, you should start with your job description. Well-written job descriptions generally have the technical and special skills listed on them. If your job descriptions don't, you may need to start the entire hiring process with a job analysis. In either case, to ensure that you have all the critical bases covered on the telephone screening interview form, you may want to use a simple fill-in-the-blank process. For example:

Candidates who do not have _____ (specific knowledge/ skill/experience/competency) do not meet the basic requirements for the position and, therefore, are not to be considered as potential candidates for the position.

Once you get the list done, you will find that some of the things you have listed can be readily found on any candidate's résumé (e.g., board certification, licensing). You would not, therefore, include these on the telephone screening interview form because the person would not even have made the cut to this point if these requirements were not found on the résumé. Once these "obvious" criteria are removed, the remaining criteria can then be used to develop the telephone interview screening form. While some of these questions may be behavior based, the primary focus of the telephone screening interview is to ascertain whether the candidate has the special/basic skills and technical background that would justify bringing her in for a face-to-face interview.

For some positions, there is a high technical component; for others, there is a high interpersonal skills component. To better look at how this mix might fall out, we can look at the mix of prequalifying factors on a matrix of interpersonal to technical skills, such as is shown in Figure 5-1.

Now, let's look at how this matrix might play out from three different quadrants. In the lower right quadrant one would find jobs that have a high interpersonal component with relatively low level technical skill expertise required. The wide range of positions one might expect to find in this quadrant includes customer service

Figure 5-1   Matrix of technical vs. interpersonal skills.

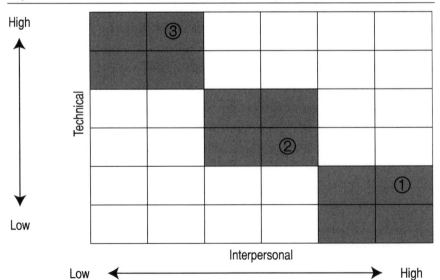

representative, administrative assistant, sales consultant, receptionist, or cashier.

Let's look more in-depth at the sales consultant position, which is shown as (1) in Figure 5-1. This particular position is in a consulting organization that brokers a wide range of consulting services (e.g., organizational development, soft skills training, computer training, quality). In this organization, the job is highly "touchy-feely," requiring that the person in the position be able to read between the lines of need, appropriately diagnose developmental needs, match needs with services, and build a solid working relationship with the client. In order to do this, the sales consultant needs to have a basic understanding of the services being sold and know which would meet the client's needs. The sales consultant is not, however, required to be competent to perform any of the services she is selling. It is, therefore, quite low on technical skills requirements.

Some of the basic requirements for the sales consultant are experience in a wide range of industries, experience selling outside the company, ability to sell non-tangibles (services versus products), a consultative sales approach, demonstrated relationship-building skills, and effective communication and listening skills. These things may not be readily apparent on a potential candidate's résumé. Since they are basic requirements, though, it would make sense to ensure that any candidate brought in for a face-to-face interview meet these needs. If you look at the Sample Telephone Screening Interview Form for sales consultant (Figure 5-2), you can see that these basic requirements can be found in the document.

You will also find, at the end of the form, a section for "other notes/comments." This section can be used to record additional, appropriate information you gathered from the candidate. For example, if in the course of answering a question, the candidate provided information indicating proficiency on a competency that is part of the interview process, the reference to that competency can be recorded in this section. A second use of this section is to record

Figure 5-2  Sample telephone screening interview form: sales consultant.

| | Excellent | Acceptable | Unacceptable |
|---|---|---|---|
| Candidate's Name _____ <br><br> Date _____ Interviewer _____ | | | |
| 1. What industries have you worked in? What percentage of time have you worked in each? | | | |
| 2. What was your role in the sales organization? [Note: e.g., support, retail, inside, external] | | | |
| 3. How would you approach a sales call with training or organizational development as your product or service? | | | |
| 4. How do you go about building a relationship with a new client/customer? | | | |
| 5. Which communication skill do you think is most important and why? | | | |
| 6. Give me an example where your ability to listen effectively and ask good questions helped you exceed a client's/customer's expectations. | | | |
| ☐ Recommend face-to-face interview with candidate <br> ☐ Recommend not pursuing candidate | | | |
| Other notes/comments: | | | |

any relevant questions or comments from the candidate. For example, if he asks about the next step in the interview process and tells you that he'll be on vacation the following week, you could record "not available for interview week of _____."

Going back to Figure 5-1, the center quadrant would contain positions that have some technical requirements, but that also require a moderate level of interpersonal skills. The absence of either would, in most situations, eliminate the candidate from consideration. Positions in this quadrant would likely include HR benefits administrator, bank loan officer, realtor, office manager, accounting manager, as well as some product sales personnel.

Let's look at the accounting manager in more detail, shown as (2) in Figure 5-1. In this particular organization, there are some technical aspects to the job of accounting manager without which it would not be productive to pursue an interview. These would include technical/special skills such as:

- Bachelor's degree in accounting
- Skilled in the use of Excel, Access, and Word
- Experience in preparing and analyzing financial statements
- P&L background
- Experience with ADP Enterprise or PeopleSoft Payroll
- Financial and accounting report-writing skills
- Previous supervisory experience of a staff of at least six employees

Since some of these requirements (e.g., B.S. in accounting or payroll package experience) would be found on the résumé, they would not be incorporated into the telephone screening interview. Likewise, you may decide not to include any technical or special skills on which you would be willing to train the person. The remaining technical and special skills, then, would be used on the telephone screening interview.

In order for a person to be successful in the position in any organization there are also a number of interpersonal or soft skills that are required. For the accounting manager position in this organization, there are four critical soft skills, without which the company would not be interested in pursuing a face-to-face interview. These include:

1. Experience and comfort with interacting effectively with top management
2. Ability to prioritize in order to meet deadlines
3. Written communication skills
4. Ethics/values/integrity

Putting this information into a telephone screening interview format, one might come up with something similar to the example for the accounting manager, as shown in Figure 5-3.

Going back to Figure 5-1, in the upper left quadrant one would find the more highly technical positions that require a relatively low level of interpersonal skills to be successful. One would probably find positions such as chemist, CAD operator, electrical engineer, or environmental technician in this quadrant. This is not to say that having good interpersonal skills might not be a hiring advantage for any of these positions (all else being equal). It simply means that one can be successful in these kinds of positions without being the belle of the ball.

Let's take a look at what a telephone screening interview format might look like for an environmental technician, shown as (3) in Figure 5-1. Unless the candidate possesses technical skills and/ or knowledge such as the following, he would not be successful in that position in this particular organization:

- B.S. in biology, chemistry, toxicology, environmental science, or related field
- Experience with the state's regulatory requirements for risk assessment

Figure 5-3   Sample telephone screening interview form: accounting manager.

| | Excellent | Acceptable | Unacceptable |
|---|---|---|---|
| Candidate's Name _____<br><br>Date _____  Interviewer _____ | | | |
| 1. Give me an example of a complex financial statement you have prepared. What made it complex? | | | |
| 2. Tell me about the most challenging experience you have had in the past couple of years writing a financial or accounting report. What made it particularly challenging? | | | |
| 3. What was the largest number of direct reports you have ever had? In what functional areas? How did you handle the different personalities? | | | |
| 4. Give me an example of a time where your attention to detail helped you avoid making a mistake or preserved the department's credibility. | | | |
| 5. Give me an example of a time where, despite being tense or nervous, you were able to make a successful presentation to a higher level management group. | | | |

*(continues)*

Figure 5-3 (Continued).

| | | | |
|---|---|---|---|
| 6. Tell me about a time you had a lot of tasks on your plate all at once. How do you decide what tasks to do and when to do them? Were there any deadlines you missed? If so, how did you handle the missed deadlines? | | | |
| 7. Give me an example of an important report you have written. What made it so important? | | | |
| 8. Tell me about a time you saw someone at work stretch or bend a rule, policy, or procedure beyond what you felt was acceptable. What did you do? Why did you take that action? | | | |
| ☐ Recommend face-to-face interview with candidate<br>☐ Recommend not pursuing candidate | | | |
| Other notes/comments: | | | |

- Experience with environmental site assessments
- HAZWOPER certification
- RCRA, CERCLA, NPDES
- Certificate for stack testing for air emission compliance
- Soil and surface water sampling and monitoring experience
- Data interpretation

What makes this job unique is a number of make-or-break job-related requirements that typically will not show up on any candidate's résumé. These include being able and willing to:

- Work in extremely hot or cold environments
- Periodically lift over twenty-five pounds
- Climb or crawl in confined spaces
- Work at heights in excess of four feet
- Wear a hazardous atmosphere respirator
- Work on call

When the interpersonal skills for success are examined for this position, we find far fewer than with the other two positions. The interpersonal skills include:

- Contractor relations
- Conflict management
- Written and oral communication skills

Putting this information onto a telephone screening interview form for this company (recognizing that it may not be the same requirements for every company with this position), the end result could look like the example for the environmental technician, as shown in Figure 5-4.

Depending on the position, there are many other factors that

Figure 5-4 Sample telephone screening interview form: environmental technician.

| | Excellent | Acceptable | Unacceptable |
|---|---|---|---|
| Candidate's Name _____<br><br>Date _____ Interviewer _____ | | | |
| 1. Tell me about the most difficult conflict you have ever had to solve with a contractor. | | | |
| 2. Sometimes there are different interpretations of the sample data between the state, industry, and public sector. Give me an example of a time you experienced this situation. How was the situation resolved? | | | |
| 3. Give me an example of a project you contracted out that had a large scope of work. | | | |
| 4. Sometimes a contractor will shortcut specs. Tell me about a time this happened to you. What did you do? What was the outcome? | | | |
| 5. Please give me an overview of the kinds of memos, forms, permits, and reports you have had to write. | | | |
| 6. What job-related training have you received outside of your degree? | | | |

| 7. There are a number of working conditions that are required for the position. As I read through them, please let me know if you are able and willing—with or without reasonable accommodations—to work under the condition I describe: | Able/willing? | |
| --- | --- | --- |
| | Yes | No |
| a. Extreme heat/cold environments | | |
| b. Climb/crawl in confined spaces | | |
| c. Work at heights in excess of 4 feet | | |
| d. Periodically lifting over 25 pounds | | |
| e. Wear a hazardous atmosphere respirator | | |
| f. Work on call | | |
| ☐ Recommend face-to-face interview with candidate<br>☐ Recommend not pursuing candidate | | |
| Other notes/comments: | | |

may need to be included in a telephone screening interview, such as being:

- Able and willing to work the hours required for the position (e.g., third shift, swing shift, an off-shift start-and-stop time)
- Able and willing to work overtime and/or weekends
- Willing to use his personal automobile for work-related travel
- Able to type within a specified typing range (e.g., 50–60 WMP)
- Able to operate a specific piece of equipment
- Fluent in another language
- Certified (e.g., Certified Internet Webmaster, SPHR/PHR, Microsoft Certified System Engineer)

When conducting a telephone interview, regardless of the basic, essential job knowledge/skills you are screening for on the form, you would take notes relative to the potential candidate's answers and then check off the appropriate rating box, or rate the candidate using another method. After the telephone screening interview, you would recommend whether to pursue a face-to-face interview with the candidate, that is, whether the candidate possesses the basic job requirements to warrant further consideration.

Throughout this chapter, the assumption has been made that the telephone screening interview is conducted one-on-one. There are organizations that have taken other approaches. The most common alternate approach is to have a second person listen in on or participate in the telephone screening interview. This person would also rate the candidate. The two interviewers would then compare notes and make a joint recommendation on whether to pursue a candidate. Organizations that have used this approach tend to report that the cost of having two people conducting the telephone screening interview is outweighed by the minimization of rater error.

Before we move off the first of the five guidelines to conducting a successful telephone screening interview, here is a warning on basic job requirements. Sometimes it is tempting to establish high requirements to attract the best candidates for the position. Be careful when establishing the requirements to do so in a nondiscriminatory manner. If you are uncertain as to the legality or appropriateness of a specific requirement, contact your legal department.

## 2. Keeping the Interview Short

A telephone screening interview is an opportunity to make sure that the potential candidate meets the basic needs and requirements for the position. As such, it should not be a full-blown interview. Generally, a telephone screening interview should be kept short and concise—typically no more than thirty minutes. Remember that your only purpose in conducting a telephone screening interview is to determine whether the potential candidate meets the basic requirements, without which it would not be of value to do a face-to-face interview.

## 3. Avoiding an In-Depth Discussion of the Job Requirements

At no point during the telephone screening interview should you discuss the specific responsibilities or required competencies of the position with the potential candidate. This information should be withheld until after you have gathered all of the data you want or need on the candidate, which would place this kind of disclosure toward the end of the first face-to-face interview. If information about the position is provided to the candidate too early, it is possible that she could answer even CBBI questions in a manner that would enable her to appear to be a stronger fit for the position than she actually is.

## 4. Conducting a Legal Interview

The telephone screening interview is part of the entire interview process; therefore, it must be legally conducted. Your documentation must be of the same appropriate nature as a face-to-face interview. Bottom line: Don't do or say anything that would be illegal in a face-to-face interview because the same rules apply. It is important to remember that when any telephone screening interview form is used that it is an interview document and that it is treated as such. Specifically, all of the notes on the document must be job-related. If you are uncertain as to any aspect of your interviewing process or forms, meet with your legal department to review your concerns.

## 5. Using the Proper Equipment

Avoid conducting the telephone screening interview over a cell phone. While this may seem like common sense to you, it's not to everyone. A friend of mine who was a candidate for a director-level position recently suffered through a telephone screening interview conducted over a recruiter's cell phone. The reception was so poor he could only hear about half of what the recruiter was saying, and kept having to ask the recruiter to repeat or clarify what she was asking. After a few minutes, my friend suggested that the interview be rescheduled for another time, the recruiter said, "That's OK. I can hear you just fine." The morale of the story: It is important not only that you be able to clearly hear and understand the candidate, but that the candidate be able to clearly hear and understand you. When you couple this problem with the dropped signals that can also plague cell phone interviews, you end up with a telephone screening interview that has so completely disrupting the interview process that it is practically worthless.

By the way, my friend was offered the director position mentioned above, but declined. While not the deciding factor, the cell phone interview did play a part in his decision.

# 6

# Creating the Interview Guide

**Every organization** designs its own interview form or guide, one that works most effectively with its culture and the needs of its interviewers. Regardless of the final form the document takes, a well-designed Interview Guide will have at least three sections:

1. Summary/overview
2. CBBI questions
3. Rating scales

This chapter examines each of these three sections of an Interview Guide and provides sample formats for each.

## 1. Summary/Overview

The Summary/Overview is a one- to two-page quick reference of all the critical information on the candidate (see Figure 6-1). While to some this section may seem to be additional, unnecessary paperwork, it can actually save time when you get to the point of comparing the ratings of one candidate to another. When all this information is clearly and neatly contained at the beginning of the interview document, there is no need to fumble through the pages of the document looking for specific ratings or notations.

As shown in Figure 6-1, the technical and special skills of the position are noted first. The logic in doing this is that this is one of

Figure 6-1    Sample interview form for [position]: summary/
overview.

Candidate _____ Interview Date _____ Interviewer _____

### 1. Technical and Special Skills

_____ (e.g., preferred degree)          Rating
_____ (e.g., certification)             Scale:
_____ (e.g., license)

| Possesses | 5 |
|---|---|
| Does Not Possess | 0 |

_____ (e.g., quality experience such as Six    Rating
Sigma)                                           Scale:
_____ (e.g., knowledge of a specific world-
class manufacturing technique)
_____ (e.g., experience working with or in a
specific industry

| Does Not Possess | 0 |
|---|---|
| Minimal | 1–2 |
| Average/Adequate | 3–4 |
| Above Average | 5–6 |
| Excellent | 7–8 |

### 2. Competencies

*Competency and Definition*                              *Rating*

_____    _____

_____    _____

_____    _____

_____    _____

_____    _____

### 3. Strength and Weaknesses

| STRENGTHS | WEAKNESSES |
|---|---|
|  |  |

OTHER COMMENTS

Recommendation

○ Recommend to hire (with satisfactory background and reference check)

○ Continue to interview—strong candidate

○ Continue to interview—need to resolve issue(s) around _____
_____

○ Recommend not hiring

○ Other (specify) _____
_____

the first items you review on a candidate's application to determine whether to proceed with an interview. In this example, there are two different rating scales used within the "Technical and Special Skills" section. The first applies to requirements that are "either/or," as in "either you have it or you don't." For example, the candidate either meets the job requirement of having a Bachelor's degree in chemical engineering or she doesn't meet that requirement. There are no shades of gray.

This kind of rating makes sense for degrees, licenses, certifications, and similar requirements. The second rating scale applies to requirements in which there is a range of acceptable fit. In the example in Figure 6-1, an eight-point Likert scale is used, with two points per descriptor. Any point distribution—from a three-point to a ten-point scale—is acceptable as long as it is easily understood by those who will be using the scale.

The next component of the Summary/Overview is the "Competencies" section. Each competency is defined according to how the company is using that term or phrase. The rating the interviewer gave the candidate on the applicable competency is also recorded on the form. Note that because not all interviewers will be assigned questions on every competency, there are likely to be some competencies for which an individual interviewer will not be rating a candidate.

The third component of the Summary/Overview is the most subjective part of the interview process. In this section, the interviewer has an opportunity to record impressions of the candidate's strengths, weaknesses, as well as other observations. It is strongly suggested, though, that each of these subjective observations be tied as closely as possible to answers the candidate provided in response to specific interview questions.

Figure 6-2 shows two very different recordings of strengths and weaknesses. The short-hand entries in the "Poor Example" could create a problem for the interviewer, when at a later review she may not remember what she was referring to when she originally made the notations. Does "+ fast paced" mean that the person works well in a fast-paced environment or that he is looking for a fast-paced work environment? Does "micromanaged?" mean that the person is a micromanager or that the person was micromanaged? The more time that has passed since the interviewer wrote these cryptic notes, the less likely it is that she will be able to explain them completely and accurately.

The "Good Example," on the other hand, provides sufficient detail to jog the interviewer's memory, enabling her to fully discuss the candidate.

## 2. CBBI Questions

The CBBI Questions are the second section found in the Interview Guide. These are the pages that contain the CBBI competencies and questions. There should be one page for each competency,

Figure 6-2   Strengths and weaknesses: poor vs. good examples.

| Poor Example | |
|---|---|
| STRENGTHS<br><br>+ fast-paced | WEAKNESSES<br><br>Micromanaged? |

| Good Example | |
|---|---|
| STRENGTHS<br><br>*High tolerance for working in a fast-paced, stressful environment. See answers to Ambiguity #2, Flexibility #1.* | WEAKNESSES<br><br>*The company the candidate currently works in is—in his words—tightly managed. Examples provided indicate that the company may be micromanaged (Competency A, #1: "Even if we know the right thing to do, management tells us to do something different." Competency C, #2: "Yes, I did ask why we were doing X instead of Y. I was to just do it; my job wasn't to ask questions." and "Following directions—explicitly—is simply the best course of action." Because of these comments, I'm concerned about his ability to function effectively in this loosely managed company.* |

allowing sufficient room for the interviewer to make appropriate interview notes.

It is not required, but it is strongly recommended that the STAR process be incorporated into the CBBI-Questions section. Because CBBI focuses on real-world experience, it is important to get all the facts relevant to the situation the candidate is presenting. The STAR process, as illustrated in Figure 6-3, guides the interviewer to do this.

Another consideration in developing each CBBI-Questions

Figure 6-3   The STAR process.

| Situation | What was the situation the candidate was faced with or what did he or she need to accomplish? What were the circumstances? |
|---|---|
| Task | What tasks did the person need to accomplish to deal with the situation? You may need to ask probing questions on the Task and Action to ensure that you are finding out what the candidate did, especially if the candidate talks about what "we" did. |
| Action | What specifically did the candidate do to accomplish the task? (NOTE: Make sure you know what the *candidate's* actions were. Some people will use phrases such as "We did . . ." or "We discovered . . ." when they didn't do anything themselves. When you hear "we" statements, make sure you follow-up and clarify. (See Chapter 4 for more information on probing/follow-up questions.) |
| Results | What was the outcome? Were the tasks accomplished? Did the actions solve the situation with which the candidate was faced? What did the candidate learn from the experience? |

page has to do with whether the rating scale is on the same page as the competency and questions or whether it is separate. Figure 6-4 illustrates a CBBI-Questions page that is set up without the rating scale. This is, of course, not the only set-up option available. The "best" setup is the one that works for the interviewers. Regardless of the format you choose to use, there should be one page for each competency. Figure 6-5 will give you a better feel for what this page might look like as part of an interview packet.

## 3. Rating Scales

The third and final section in a well-designed Interview Guide is the rating scales. There are two primary options for rating scales. One is developing a form where the rating scale is part of the CBBI-Questions page. The second primary option is to have a separate document for the rating scales. This can either be a completely separate document or a page following the CBBI interview questions.

In addition to the organization's culture, the biggest factor in

Figure 6-4    CBBI questions: competency format.

Candidate _____    Interview Date _____

Competency: (listed and defined with desired behaviors)

| (Behavioral interview question #1) |
|---|
| Situation    Task    Action    Results |

| (Behavioral interview question #2) |
|---|
| Situation    Task    Action    Results |

determining how to incorporate the rating scale is the design of the rating scales, which are often referred to as *behaviorally anchored ratings scales* (BARS) or *behavioral observation scales* (BOS).

Rating scales can range from very simple scales that apply universally to all competencies to very complex and detailed scales that apply to each specific competency. In their purest sense, a BARS or BOS will reduce rater discrepancies by linking a numerical rating with specific and defined behaviors at various points along the rating scale.

The more detailed and structured the BARS or BOS, the greater the consistency tends to be across raters on the same competency for the same candidate. That is, if two people interview a single candidate on a single competency, the more clearly defined the

Figure 6-5   CBBI questions: "planning" competency.

Candidate: <u>John Doe</u>                    Interview Date: <u>5/8/200X</u>

**Competency: Planning**—Able to lay the groundwork to ensure that critical tasks, projects, goals, and objectives are accomplished within the agreed-upon timeframe.

- ☐ Accurately anticipates length and difficulty of tasks and projects
- ☐ Sets objectives and goals
- ☐ Breaks task/project down into bite-sized pieces, utilizing an effective process to developed a time table and make task-people assignments
- ☐ Is able to anticipate problems and roadblocks and make appropriate adjusts
- ☐ Measures performance against goals; evaluates results

| Give me an example of an idea you tried to sell to management that was not adopted? <br> • Why do you think it wasn't adopted? <br> • If you had it to do over again, what would you do differently? |
|---|
| Situation    Task    Action    Results |

NOTES:

| Give me an example of a time you had to accomplish something without sufficient information, guidelines, or direction. |
|---|
| Situation    Task    Action    Results |

NOTES:

scale, the more likely the interviewers are to agree on the rating for the candidate. The drawback to this specificity is, however, that developing this kind of competency-by-competency detail can be very frustrating, arduous, and time consuming. With that said, it must be remembered that this is a one-time effort. Once the time has been put in to develop a specific rating scale for a competency, the rating scale would apply to every position with that competency across the organization.

That does not mean that the specific competency rating scale is always the best choice. What is best will depend upon the organization's culture, practices, and overall approach to interviewing. Let's look at this range of options, starting with the most basic rating scale.

### The Bare-Bones, One-Scale-Fits-All-Competencies Rating Scale

The scale in Figure 6-6 is an example of a very basic rating scale that one could apply to all competencies. While the example uses a 6-point Likert scale, any numbered Likert scale could be used (e.g., 1 to 4, or 0 to 10). The scale could either be incorporated in each page of the Interview Guide or it could be placed in the Summary/Overview section.

A universally applied rating scale is quick and easy to develop and use. However, it can lead to significant rating disagreements

Figure 6-6  Basic rating scale: 6-point Likert scale.

| 0 | 1–2 | 3–4 | 5–6 |
|---|---|---|---|
| Does not meet basic requirement | Meets the basic requirement | Slightly exceeds the basic requirement | Significantly exceeds the basic requirement |
| Notes on Rating: | | | |

between raters. For example, let's say that we are interviewing a candidate on the competency "effective listening skills." I may believe that anyone who has the patience to sit and listen to another human being for more than five seconds without fiddling with something on their desk and who periodically makes eye contact with the speaker is demonstrating outstanding listening skills. You, on the other hand (being a highly trained, skilled, talented manager), believe that active listening means that the person maintains eye contact, uses paraphrasing to check for understanding, asks questions to gain a better understanding, and uses nonverbals effectively and appropriately. If we used the scale in Figure 6-6, it is highly likely that the two of us would rate any given candidate very differently. When it comes to discussing the candidate, we would be likely to have a very "active" conversation about where the candidate should really be rated on the "listening" competency.

If we bump the scale up a bit, we can still look at a one-size-fits-all-competencies approach, but one that will give interviewers slightly more direction. Figure 6-7 (using a $-1$ to 4 scale) and Figure 6-8 (using a 0 to 8 scale) show more detailed approaches.

### Rating Scale Keyed to Each Competency

To get any more specific, one has to move into a competency-by-competency rating scale. Figure 6-9 provides a sample fill-in-the-blank format that could be customized for each competency. These rating scales would then either be incorporated into the interview form or provided as a separate document for the interviewer.

The most significant disadvantage to incorporating individual competency rating scales into the interview packet is that it could result in the interviewer carrying a modest-sized—and intimidating—tome into the interview. On the other hand, keeping these rating scales as separate documents means that the interviewer could make assumptions about how each rating level reads without referring to the actual wording of the rating, resulting in rating

Figure 6-7   One-size-fits-all rating scale: 4-point Likert scale.

| Rating | | Description |
|---|---|---|
| −1 | Negative | The situation described as a positive example was inconsistent with Company's definition of proficient performance of this competency.<br><br>OR<br><br>When relating a negative example, either no learning occurred from the situation or the learning was inconsistent with Company's definition of proficient performance of this competency. |
| 0 | Absent | The candidate was unable to provide an example. |
| 1 | Somewhat Effective | The candidate demonstrated most of the indicators for successful performance in this competency; the example was relatively acceptable; candidate could, with coaching/development, meet the competency as defined. |
| 2 | Proficient | The candidate successfully demonstrated the competency as defined by the Company; the candidate's example indicates an ability to successfully employ the knowledge/skills/abilities required to effectively perform this competency. |
| 3 | Excellent | The candidate described handling this situation in a manner that exceeds expectations; the described behavior went beyond the Company's definition for proficient performance in concrete measurable or observable ways. |
| 4 | Leader | The example provided by the candidate indicates that he or she would be considered a role model for others. He or she would be able to lead, train, and motivate others to be excellent in the competency. |
| Rating Notes: | | |

Figure 6-8   One-size-fits-all rating scale: 8-point Likert scale.

| Rating | Description |
|---|---|
| 7–8<br><br>Far Exceeds | • Described behavior exceeds all reasonable expectations<br>• Behavior is of a rare quality, found only in a small percentage of people in organizations<br>• Clearly recognized as being consistently distinguished in skills/ knowledge/behavior/understanding/usage<br>• Demonstrates a very high degree of expertise<br>• Would serve as a model of excellence or as a coach to others<br>• The candidate's proficiency on this competency compares with the best this company has seen |
| 5–6<br><br>Exceeds | • The candidate's described performance clearly and consistently exceeds that of a fully proficient person<br>• The candidate's answer indicates that performance is above the expected level in fulfilling the competencies for the position<br>• The candidate demonstrated unusual proficiency in handling the situation |
| 3–4<br><br>Proficient | • The candidate's described performance/behavior/skill utilization is consistent with that of an individual who is proficient in the competency.<br>• The related incident indicates that the candidate understands the criteria for success in demonstrating this competency |
| 1–2<br><br>Needs to Improve | • The candidate's description of the application of the competency is slightly below the standards acceptable for this organization<br>• Information was provided by the candidate that indicates learning has occurred from the incident and development has occurred, but not yet to Company standards |
| 0<br><br>Not Acceptable | • The candidate was unable to provide an acceptable example of the utilization of the competency<br><br>OR<br><br>• The example provided by the candidate fell substantially short of the proficient level of performance on the competency<br>• The candidate did not indicate any learning from the situation and/ or felt that his/her performance was acceptable |
| Comments Justifying Rating: | |

Figure 6-9  Competency-by-competency rating scale.

| COMPETENCY: | | | RATING: |
|---|---|---|---|
| DEFINITION: | | | |
| −1 | Negative | Evidence gathered indicating candidate's ability to _____ is severely lacking. | |
| 0 | Absent | The candidate was unable to provide an example of his/her ability to develop employees. | |
| 1–2 | Somewhat Effective | The candidate has made a few minor missteps and is, therefore, less than proficient; however he/she recognizes his/her errors, took corrective action, and learned from his/her mistakes; development has occurred and the candidate's potential for continued development is evident. | |
| 3–4 | Proficient | • <br> • | • <br> • |
| 5–6 | Excellent/ Leader | • Is a role model for others. <br> • Mentors others. | • <br> • |
| Reason for Rating: | | | |

errors. A happy medium might be to remove the rating space from the interview document and provide the interview with two separate documents: an interview form and a rating form.

An example of how this might look when it is completed for the "staff development" competency is shown in Figure 6-10.

### Competency and Rating Layout

As mentioned earlier, there are two primary choices on how to lay out the interview form in terms of the CBBI questions and the rating scale: combined or separate. To help you determine which might be the best choice for your organization, Figures 6-11 to 6-16 present examples of different layouts.

Combined competency and rating layout examples can be

Figure 6-10  "Staff development" competency: rating scale.

| Competency: Staff Development | | Rating: |
|---|---|---|
| Definition: fosters the short- and long-term growth and development of direct reports through OJT, mentoring, coaching, classroom, online, and other appropriate avenues. | | |
| −1<br>Negative | Evidence gathered indicating candidate's ability to grow and develop his/her staff is severely lacking; evidence supplied by the candidate indicate either clearly inappropriate development measures were employed or the results were negative in some other manner | |
| 0<br>Absent | The candidate was unable to provide an example of his/her ability to develop employees | |
| 1–2<br>Somewhat Effective | The candidate has made a few minor missteps and is, therefore, less than proficient; however he/she recognizes his/her errors, took corrective action, and learned from his/her mistakes; development has occurred and the candidate's potential for continued development is evident | |
| 3–4<br>Proficient | • Believes that employee development is a critical part of his/her job<br>• Provides constructive feedback (not criticism)<br>• Knows the career goals of each of his/her direct reports<br>• Designs and executes, with employee input, a developmental plan for each employee<br>• Holds developmental review and planning meetings twice a year with each employee | • Is able to determine the most appropriate method for staff development, with or without input from the OD department<br>• Has a track record of providing direct reports with opportunities for growth within their positions as well as outside their positions |
| 5–6<br>Excellent/ Leader | • Is a role model for others<br>• Mentors others<br>• Holds at least quarterly developmental review and planning meetings with each employee | • Will hire, or accept in transfer, an employee who has potential, but needs some coaching/mentoring |
| Specific Examples to Explain Rating: | | |

found for the competencies "giving/receiving information" (Figure 6-11) and "values diversity" (Figure 6-12). Separate competency and rating sheets can be found for the competencies "ethics and integrity" (Figures 6-13 and 6-14) and "results oriented" (Figures 6-15 and 6-16).

*(text continues on page 145)*

Figure 6-11   Competency and rating format for "giving/receiving information."

| COMPETENCY & DEFINITION: *Giving/Receiving Information.* Maintains open lines of communication up, down, and across the organization, as well as inside and outside the organization. | | | | |
|---|---|---|---|---|
| Behaviors | | | | |
| • Obtains input from others as and when appropriate | ? | — | √ | + |
| • Expresses opinions, views, and ideas in a non-threatening manner | ? | — | √ | + |
| • Ensure that the opinions, values, and ideas of others are heard | ? | — | √ | + |
| • Provides timely updates | ? | — | √ | + |
| • Ensures people have the necessary information to work effectively | ? | — | √ | + |
| • Uses the appropriate communication vehicle | ? | — | √ | + |
| Q1: Tell me about a situation where, because you had a strong network, you were able to gather information that others were not able to secure. | | | | |
| Q2: Describe a situation where you delayed providing someone with information that would have been valuable to them. | | | | |
| NOTES: | | | | S T A R |
| Competency Rating: | ☐ 4—Leader<br>☐ 3—Exceed<br>☐ 2—Met<br>☐ 1—Nearly Met<br>☐ 0—Not Demonstrated | | | |

Figure 6-12   Competency and rating format for "values diversity."

| Competency: VALUES DIVERSITY | | Rating: |
|---|---|---|
| *Unacceptable (0)* | • Doesn't deal well with people different from self<br>• Uncomfortable with differences between people<br>• Doesn't see business value of diversity<br>• Stereotypes people/groups | |
| *Proficient (3)* | • Handles diversity issues in timely and appropriate manner<br>• Hires for talent and potential without regard to race, national-ity, culture, disability, and/or gender<br>• Conforms to and supports all company policies, procedures, and guidelines on diversity | |
| *Exceptional (6)* | Proficient plus:<br>• Proactive in addressing diversity<br>• Actively seeks out and recruits a diverse workforce<br>• Models inclusive behavior<br>• Actively seeks out opportunities to work with individuals differ-ent from self<br>• Coaches others on diversity issues | |
| Q1: Tell me about a time you adapted your style in order to work effectively with those who were different from you. | | Q2: Tell me about a time you took action to make someone feel comfortable in an environment that was obviously uncom-fortable with his or her presence. |
| NOTES: | | NOTES: |

Figure 6-13  "Ethics and integrity" competency: sample questions.

| COMPETENCY: ETHICS & INTEGRITY—Relies on a solid set of core values to provide guidance through good and bad times; behaves in ways that engender trust and respect. |
|---|
| Tell me about a specific time when you had to handle a tough problem that challenged fairness or ethical issues. |
| Situation     Task     Action     Results |
| NOTES: |

| Tell me about a time you saw someone at work stretch or bend a rule, policy, or procedure beyond what you felt was acceptable. |
|---|
| Situation     Task     Action     Results |
| NOTES: |

Figure 6-14  "Ethics and integrity" competency: rating sheet.

| |
|---|
| ETHICS & INTEGRITY—Relies on a solid set of core values to provide guidance through good and bad times; behaves in ways that engender trust and respect. |

- ○ Adheres to Company's Code of Ethics and Integrity
- ○ Keeps promises
- ○ Maintains confidentiality
- ○ Admits mistakes
- ○ Provides honest, helpful feedback
- ○ Does not overlook inappropriate or marginally inappropriate behavior in others; handles in an effective, timely manner
- ○ Exemplifies the highest standards of honesty, integrity, and ethical business behavior
- ○ Practices what he/she preaches
- ○ Holds self and others accountable for acting with integrity and being ethical

RATING

☐ Example provided was unethical or failed to meet the above behavioral descriptors. Explain:

☐ Example demonstrated compliance with only a few of the above behavioral descriptors. Explain:

☐ Example demonstrated the majority of the above behavioral descriptors, as marked.

☐ Example demonstrated most, if not all, the above behavioral descriptors (as marked). The candidate would be an excellent ethics and integrity coach/leader/mentor.

Figure 6-15  "Results oriented" competency: sample
questions.

---

RESULTS ORIENTED: Focuses on achieving—or exceeding—goals; has a propensity
toward action and accomplishment.

#1: Tell me about a time when you were asked to complete a difficult assignment and
the odds were against you. What did you learn from the experience?

#2: (optional) Tell me about a time when you did *not* achieve the results you should
have or in the timeframe you should have.

| #1 | |
|---|---|
| Situation | |
| Task | |
| Action | |
| Results | |
| #2 | |
| Situation | |
| Task | |
| Action | |
| Results | |

Regardless of the rating scale used, there should be some place
on the form (preferably near the rating scale) for the candidate to
make notes relative to why the interviewer rated the candidate at
a specific level. Let's assume that the notes the interviewer made
for the "composure" competency are as follows:

Gave a good example. Lots of experience. No problem answering follow-up
questions. Obviously got this one down!

What's the primary problem with this? Even if there is only
one day—and a couple of interviews—between writing this com-

Figure 6-16  "Results oriented" competency: rating sheet.

| RESULTS ORIENTED | | | |
|---|---|---|---|
| Behaviors: | | | |
| ☐ Demonstrated strong personal sense of purpose | | | |
| ☐ Set/accepted challenging goal | | | |
| ☐ Focused on getting the desired/expected results | | | |
| ☐ Conveyed an appropriate sense of urgency for the situation | | | |
| ☐ Persisted/persevered in the face of obstacles and roadblocks | | | |
| ☐ Didn't procrastinate; brought closure to the task/project within agreed-upon timeframe | | | |
| ☐ Maintained a high level of productivity | | | |
| ☐ Focused on the critical few rather than the trivial many | | | |
| ☐ Demonstrated high personal standards of achievement (standards of excellence) | | | |
| ☐ Monitored own progress and provided updates to appropriate person(s) | | | |
| ☐ Demonstrated a willingness to make the personal sacrifices necessary to be successful | | | |

| NOTES: | Rating | | |
|---|---|---|---|
| | Exceptional | 6 | 7 |
| | Proficient | 4 | 5 |
| | Marginal | 2 | 3 |
| | Unacceptable | 0 | 1 |

ment and meeting to make the final hiring decision, chances are that the interviewer will not be able to remember what the "good example" was and what it was that indicated that the candidate has "got this one down."

As part of their training, all interviewers should be taught how to write specific, effective, job-related rating notes. For example:

Presentation to board. Not all charts had been updated by staff—forgot to check (accepted responsibility). Didn't know some information a board member asked—got "ripped apart" (deep breathing, listening). Handled department-related questions outside of material being presented (using appropriate humor—e.g., question on future of department). Volunteered what was learned (planning, checking work, practice presenting, anticipate related/unrelated questions) from this situation and how incorporated learning into future presentations.

Notes like this record the specific details of the situation and provide reminders as to why the interviewer rated the candidate at a particular level. Even if there are events occurring between the interviews and the discussion of the candidates, with such detailed notes the interviewer is more likely to be able to remember the specifics of the candidate's situation and to fully discuss why he was rated at a particular level.

$7$ ................................................

# Assembling the Interviewer
# Data

**Too often** when there are multiple interviewers, everyone has their own form, their own perspective as to which competencies are most critical, their own way of asking questions, and their own way of rating performance. Then, when the interviewers sit down to discuss each candidate, it becomes a lot like the process of comparing apples and oranges.

This chapter presents two forms that will help increase the chances that you are comparing apples to apples. The first form, the Individual Candidate Rating Form (Figure 7-1), combines the ratings of all of the interviewers for a single candidate.

The information for the Skills and Competencies column (1) comes off of the first page of the interview sheet. This is simply a cut-and-paste process.

In the middle section (2), the interviewers' initials are recorded along with their individual ratings for those skills or competencies they covered during their interview. In most situations, not all interviewers will ask questions on all the skills or competencies for a position. Where multiple interviewer ratings are available, they are averaged for each skill and each competency, and the average for each is recorded in the Average column (3).

Once an Individual Candidate Rating Form has been completed on each candidate, a cumulative report—the Comparison of Candi-

Figure 7-1   Individual Candidate Rating: sample form.

Candidate _____ Position _____

| ① Skills & Competencies | ② Interviewers' Initials | | | ③ Average |
|---|---|---|---|---|
| **Technical & Special Skills** | *Rating* | *Rating* | *Rating* | |
| | | | | |
| | | | | |
| | | | | |
| | | | | |
| | | | | |
| **Competencies** | | | | |
| | | | | |
| | | | | |
| | | | | |
| | | | | |
| | | | | |
| | | | | |
| | | | | |
| | | | | |
| | | | | |

dates Form (Figure 7-2)—is assembled, enabling a side-by-side, quantitative comparison of the candidates.

Once again, the information for the Skills and Competencies column (1) comes off of the first page of the interview sheet. At the top of the right columns, the name of each candidate is recorded (2). Finally, the average rating for each candidate's skills and competencies is copied off each Individual Candidate Rating Form and recorded in the appropriate columns (3).

Once the information is assembled on this form, a discussion can be held about each of the candidates. It can then be decided who should be offered the position, pending any background check, reference check, or other organizational hiring requirements.

Figure 7-2   Comparison of Candidates: sample form.

| ① Skills & Competencies | Candidates' Names ② | | | |
|---|---|---|---|---|
| | ③ Average Rating | | | |
| **Technical & Special Skills** | | | | |
| | | | | |
| | | | | |
| | | | | |
| | | | | |
| **Competencies** | | | | |
| | | | | |
| | | | | |
| | | | | |
| | | | | |
| | | | | |
| | | | | |
| | | | | |

# Where Do You Go from Here?

**Now that you have established** competencies and are hiring candidates against them, it makes sense to start incorporating the competencies into your other human resource programs and processes. In this chapter we will briefly look at some of the next competency-integration steps you could take.

## Performance Management

One of the many reasons employees dislike annual performance reviews is that they feel the review is arbitrary and capricious. They may view it as something that is being done to them that really has little importance or value rather than seeing it as a tool that can be used to help them improve in their position and grow with the organization.

Competencies can change that mindset. When individual performance is linked to business performance, the organization's performance management process begins to take on a value in the organization. Employees start to see the link between their day-to-day work activities and the organization achieving its mission, vision, and strategic plan—as well as operating in accordance with its values and ethics statements. Besides, it only makes sense that if you are going to hire people according to competencies that you also evaluate their performance against those same competencies.

What the actual performance management forms look like may

well differ for non-exempt and exempt employees. Let's look at the basic requirements for each.

*Non-Exempt Employees*

It is recommended that, at a minimum, the form for non-exempt employees contain sections for:

1. *Competencies with BARS and Rating Scales.* In most organizations, this section is significantly more straightforward than what one would find with an exempt position. Figure 8-1 illustrates a competency with rating, excerpted from a non-exempt performance review.

2. *Accomplishments/Achievements.* Even though ongoing feedback is an integral part of effective performance management, too often we forget to tell our direct reports about the good things that they have accomplished during the year. This section is a reminder to either point these things out or summarize the positive feedback you have given the employee during the course of the year.

3. *Areas for Improvement.* This section details what needs to be improved, how it needs to be improved, and by when.

Figure 8-1  Competency with rating: excerpt from non-exempt performance review.

| QUALITY OF WORK. CONSIDER THE ABILITY AND ACCURACY TO PRODUCE ACCEPTED WORK THAT MEETS COMPANY STANDARDS. | | | | |
|---|---|---|---|---|
| Very few errors. Does high quality work consistently. Data accuracy is high. | Seldom makes errors. Work is usually correct with few errors and is of good quality. Data accuracy is good. | Quality is above minimum standards. Occasionally makes errors but seldom repeats after correction. Data accuracy is acceptable. | Work often needs regular inspection. Makes more errors than should. | Makes excessive and repetitive mistakes. Cannot be given work requiring accuracy. |
| *Far Exceeds* | *Exceeds* | *Meets* | *Needs Improvement* | *Unacceptable* |
| | | | | |

4. *Summary/Overall.* This section contains any summary comments you wish to make, a place for the employee to comment, as well as an overall performance rating. An example of what this might look like for an hourly position is shown in Figure 8-2.

5. *Sign-Offs.* This section is where appropriate signatures and dates are recorded.

### Exempt Employees

For exempt employees, it is recommended that sections such as the following also be included:

• *Individual Goals.* These goals should be set using the familiar SMART format, which is that goals should be Specific, Measurable, Achievable, Realistic, and Time-Bound.

Figure 8-2   Performance summary for an hourly position.

| Overall Performance Summary and Rating | | | | |
|---|---|---|---|---|
| Supervisor Comments: | | | | |
| Employee Comments: | | | | |
| Outstanding overall performance. Employee consistently performs job-related tasks at high levels of competency. | High level of achievement. Employee clearly demonstrates the ability to excel in job-related tasks. | Acceptable level of performance. Employee generally meets the expectations. | Minimum level of performance. There are a number of areas in which improvement is needed. | Unsatisfactory level of performance. Significant improvement in many areas must be demonstrated quickly. |
| *Far Exceeds* | *Exceeds* | *Meets* | *Needs Improvement* | *Unacceptable* |
| | | | | |

• *Summary/Overall.* As with the non-exempt form, this section is the place for the leader and employee to make overall comments.

• *Training/Development Plan.* This section includes any goal or performance factor on which the employee did not meet expectations, any additional training/development she needs to meet current or future expectations in her present position, and any training/development required for a position into which she may be moved or promoted within the next eighteen months. It would NOT include a development plan for significant performance problems or succession planning.

Regardless of what the actual exempt form looks like, integrating competencies into your company's performance management process ensure that performance is being measured against the competencies that have been determined to be critical for success in the position and/or the organization. An example of how this might look on an actual form is illustrated in Figure 8-3.

Incorporating competencies into the performance management process is a first step in getting everyone in the organization to understand that they play an important part in the organization's overall success. This in turn leads to benefits including:

• Improved business results
• Motivated employees
• Higher morale
• Increased productivity
• A strong, solid base of high-performing employees

## Individual Performance Improvement Plans

When an employee's performance does not meet expectations, development plans can be created—either through the performance management process or as a separate document. Such plans identify the development that needs to occur and the competency to

Figure 8-3 Competencies integrated into exempt performance review form.

| | |
|---|---|
| DEVELOPS EMPLOYEES. Provides challenging/stretching tasks/assignments. Holds frequent development discussions. Is aware of direct reports' career goals. Constructs and executes compelling development plans. Pushes direct reports to accept developmental moves. Accepts direct reports who need improvement/development. Is a people builder. Completes timely performance reviews. | ☐ Far Exceeds<br>☐ Exceeds<br>☐ Solid Performance<br>☐ Needs Improvement<br>☐ Unacceptable |
| *Rationale for Rating if other than "Solid Performance"* | |
| PLANNING, ORGANIZING, AND SETTING PRIORITIES. Accurately scopes out projects. Sets SMART goals and objectives. Breaks work into bite-sized process steps. Develops clear, specific schedules and people/task assignments. Anticipates and adjusts for problems. Measures performance against goals. Can bring together resources to get things done. Able to multitask. Uses resources effectively and efficiently. Spends own time and time of others on critical few and puts trivial many aside. Eliminates roadblocks. Creates focus. | ☐ Far Exceeds<br>☐ Exceeds<br>☐ Solid Performance<br>☐ Needs Improvement<br>☐ Unacceptable |
| *Rationale for Rating if other than "Solid Performance"* | |

which the development relates. In general, the more specific each item on the development plan is—particularly in respect to what acceptable performance "looks like"—the more likely it is that the person will be able to model the competency at the required level.

## Training and Development

Training and development curriculums or individual programs can be developed and provided to ensure that employees have the skills necessary to demonstrate the competency to the required level.

An example of a progressive skill level training and development opportunity is shown in Figure 8-4.

## Succession Planning

Succession planning used to be easy. The CEO decided who would be slotted into what position, based on hunches, instincts, intuition, and, quite often, politics. Today, if it is done well, succession planning isn't that easy. Having a succession plan—and consistently monitoring, modifying, and updating it—is probably one of the most important components of building an organization that is capable of achieving its strategic plan and goals.

To be effective and valued, succession planning must be a formal, ongoing, systematic, and dynamic effort that ensures that the right people, with the right skills, are in the right place, at the right time, and ready to assume a new leadership position in the organization. When succession planning is done against the orga-

Figure 8-4   Sample progressive skill level training and development opportunity.

| Training/Development Opportunity for *Hiring/Staffing* Competency | | |
|---|---|---|
| *Level 1* | *Level 2* | *Level 3* |
| Attend an approved CBBI program. | Work with a recruiter to develop your skills. Process: 1. Observe the recruiter during at least two interviews; debrief each afterward. 2. Co-interview at least three candidates with recruiter; debrief each afterwards. 3. Interview at least three candidates while the recruiter observes; debrief each afterwards. | Participate as an interviewer during two campus recruiting sessions. Follow-up debrief with recruiter(s) who attended each session. |

nization's competency model(s), future leaders are assessed, selected, and developed with the future of the organization in mind.

Competencies blend in well with virtually any approach that a company takes to succession planning. When competency-based succession planning is done well, the process is:

- Aligned with the business strategy and its goals and objectives
- Supported by the organization's culture, vision, mission, and values
- Integrated with other HR processes

Thus, when competency-based HR systems are developed and used consistently throughout the organization, they link employees to the company's tactical and strategic direction. This consistency sends a strong message throughout the organization as to what is required for individual and organization success. The end result, then, is that individuals and organizations not only survive, but thrive, in today's competitive environment.

# Interviewing, Competencies, Competency-Based Interviewing, and Behavior-Based Interviewing

**There are, combined,** literally thousands of books, white papers, journal articles, and Internet articles on these topics. Although each article has something to offer, it would be impossible to list all of the resources here. Following, though, are a few resources to help you enhance various aspects of your recruitment, interviewing, and hiring process.

## Books

Arthur, Diane. *Recruiting, Interviewing, Selecting & Orienting New Employees, 4th ed*. New York: AMACOM, 2006.

Ball, Frederick W. and Barbara B. Ball. *Impact Hiring: The Secrets of Hiring a Superstar*. Upper Saddle River, N.J.: Prentice Hall, 2000.

Camp, Richard R., Mary E. Vielhaber, and Jack L. Simonetti. *Strategic Interviewing*. San Francisco: Jossey-Bass, 2001.

Campbell, Andrew and Kathleen Sommers Luchs. *Core Competency-Based Strategy*. Stamford, Conn.: International Thomson Business Press, 1997.

161

Cohen, David S. *The Talent Edge: A Behavioral Approach to Hiring, Developing, and Keeping Top Performers.* New York: John Wiley & Sons, 2001.

Deems, Richard S. *Interviewing: More Than a Gut Feeling.* Franklin Lakes, N.J.: Career Press, 1995.

Dipboye, R.L. "Structured and Unstructured Selection Interviews: Beyond the Job-Fit Model." In Ferris, G.R. (ed.). *Research in Personnel and Human Resources Management: Vol. 12.* Greenwich, Conn.: JAI Press, 1994.

Falcone, Paul. *96 Great Interview Questions to Ask Before You Hire.* New York: AMACOM, 1997.

———. *The Hiring and Firing Question and Answer Book.* New York: AMACOM, 2002.

Fear, Richard A. and Bob Chiron. *The Evaluation Interview: How to Probe Deeply, Get Candid Answers, and Predict the Performance of Job Candidates.* New York: McGraw-Hill, 2002.

Fry, Ron. *Ask the Right Questions, Hire the Best People.* Franklin Lakes, N.J.: Career Press, 2000.

Kador, John. *The Managers Book of Questions: 751 Great Interview Questions for Hiring the Best Person.* New York: McGraw-Hill, 1997.

Sachs, Randi Toler. *How to Become a Skillful Interviewer.* New York: AMACOM, 1994.

Spencer, Lyle M. and M. Signe. *Competence at Work: Models for Superior Performance.* New York: John Wiley & Sons, 1993.

Wendover, Robert W. *Smart Hiring: The Complete Guide to Finding and Hiring the Best Employees, 2nd ed.* Naperville, Ill.: Sourcebooks, 1998.

Wood, Robert and Tim Payne. *Competency Based Recruitment and Selection: A Practical Guide.* Chichester, U.K.: John Wiley & Sons, 1998.

## White Papers

Nemerov, Donald S. and Stephen Schoonover. "Competency-Based HR Applications Survey: Executive Summary of Results." Alexandria, Va.: Society for Human Resources Management: *SHRM White Paper*, 2001.

Pritchard, Kenneth H. "Introduction to Competencies." Alexandria, Va.: Society for Human Resources Management: *SHRM White Paper*, 1997.

Sommer, Roger D. "Behavioral Interviewing." Alexandria, Va.: Society for Human Resources Management: *SHRM White Paper*, 1998.

## Articles

These articles on the behavior- and competency-based interviewing process will give you an idea about just how a wide variety of business journals publish information on the subject.

Bradley, Elizabeth. "Hiring the Best." *Women in Business* 55.4 (July/August 2003).

Campion, Michael A., James E. Campion, and J. P. Hudson. "Structured Interviewing: A Note on Incremental Validity and Alternative Question Types." *Journal of Applied Psychology* 79 (1994).

Campion, Michael A., David K. Palmer, and James E. Campion. "A Review of Structure in the Selection Interview." *Personnel Psychology* 50 (1997), pp. 655–702.

Campion, Michael A., E. D. Pursell, and B. K. Brown. "Structured Interviewing: Raising the Psychometric Properties of the Employment Interview." *Personnel Psychology* 41 (1988), pp. 25–42.

Conway, J. M., R. A. Jako, and D. F. Goodman. (1995). "A Meta-Analysis of Interrater and Internal Consistency Reliability of Selection Interviews." *Journal of Applied Psychology* 80 (1995), pp. 565–579.

Fay, C. H. and G. P. Latham. "Effect of Training and Rating Scales on Rating Errors." *Personnel Psychology* 35 (1982), pp. 105–116.

Graves, L. M. and R. J. Karren. "The Employee Selection Interview: A Fresh Look at an Old Problem." *Human Resource Management* 35 (1996), pp. 163–180.

Harris, M. M. "Reconsidering the Employment Interview: A Review of Recent Literature and Suggestions for Future Research." *Personnel Psychology* 42 (1989), pp. 691–726.

Hirshman, Carolyn. "Playing the High-Stakes Hiring Game. *HR Magazine* 43.4 (March 1998).

Holdeman, John B. and Jeffrey M. Aldridge. "How to Hire Ms./Mr. Right." *Journal of Accountancy* 182.2 (August 1996).

Howard, J. L. and G. R. Ferris. "The Employment Interview Context: Social and Situational Influence on Interviewer Decisions." *Journal of Applied Social Psychology* 26 (1996), 112–136.

Huffcut, A. I. and W. Arthur. "Hunter and Hunter (1984) Revisited: Interview Validity for Entry-Level Jobs." *Journal of Applied Psychology* 79 (1994), pp. 184–190.

Hunter, J. E. and R. F. Hunter. "Validity and Utility of Alternative Predictors of Job Performance." *Psychological Bulletin* 96 (1984), pp. 72–98.

Isaacs, Nora. "Enterprise Career: Use Job Interviews to Evaluate 'Soft Skills.'" *Info World* (April 6, 1998).

Janz, T. "Initial Comparisons of Patterned Behavior Description Interviews Versus Unstructured Interviews." *Journal of Applied Psychology* 67 (1982), pp. 577–580.

Kelly, Maura. "The New Job Interview." *Rolling Stone* (March 15, 2001), p. 67.

Maurer, S. D. and C. Fay. "Effect of Situational Interviews, Conventional Structured Interviews, and Training on Interview Rating Agreement: An Experimental Analysis." *Personnel Psychology* 41 (1988), pp. 329–347.

McDaniel, M. A., D. L. Whetzel, F. L. Schmidt, and S. D. Maurer. "The Validity of Employment Interviews: A Comprehensive Review and Meta-Analysis." *Journal of Applied Psychology* 79 (1994), pp. 599–616.

Motowidlo, S. J., et al. "Studies of the Structured Behavioral Interview." *Journal of Applied Psychology* 5 (1992), pp. 571–587.

Pascarella, Stephen E. "Making the Right Hire: Behavioral Interviewing." *Tax Advisor* 37.9 (September/October 1996).

Pulakos, E. D., and N. Schmitt. "Experience-Based and Situational

Interview Questions: Studies of Validity." *Personnel Psychology* 48 (1995), pp. 289–308.

Schmidt, Frank L. and John E. Hunter. "The Validity and Utility of Selection Methods in Personnel Psychology: Practical and Theoretical Implications of 85 Years of Research Findings." The American Psychological Association. *Psychological Bulletin* 24.2 (September 1998).

Trotsky, Judith. "Oh, Will You Behave?" *Computerworld* 35.2 (January 8, 2001).

Watterson, Thomas. "More Employers Using Job Interview As a Test of Applicants' Mettle." *Boston Globe*, Boston Works section, September 12, 2004. (*Note*: While the article is good, the questions at the end of the article are, for the most part, *not* behavior-based.)

Weekley, J. A. and J. A. Gier. "Reliability and Validity of the Situational Interview for a Sales Position." *Journal of Applied Psychology* 72 (1987), pp. 484–487.

Wiesner, W. H. and S. F. Cronshaw. "A Meta-Analysis Investigation of the Impact of Interview Format and Degree of Structure on the Validity of the Employment Interview." *Journal of Occupational Psychology* 61 (1989), pp. 275–290.

Wright, Daisy. "Tell Stories, Get Hired." *Office Pro* 65.6 (August/September 2004).

———. "Interview Questions That Hit the Mark." *Harvard Business Review* 6.3 (March 2001).

Wright, P. M., P. A. Lichtenfels, and E. D. Pursell. "The Structured Interview: Additional Studies and a Meta-Analysis." *Journal of Occupational Psychology* 62 (1989), pp. 191–199.

Zedeck, S., A. Tziner, and S. Middlestadt. "Interview Validity and Reliability: An Individual Analysis Approach." *Personnel Psychology* 36 (1983), pp. 355–370.

# Index